YOU WERE HIT. NOW WHAT?

A Trial Lawyer's Guide to Handling Your Own Car Crash Case

Glenn B. Fair, Esq.

Trial Attorney | Fair Squared Injury Law

Licensed in Colorado and Wyoming

You Were Hit. Now What? A Trial Lawyer's Guide to Handling Your Own Car Crash Case

Published by Fair Squared

56 Inverness Drive East, Suite 235
Englewood, Colorado 80112
www.Fair2Law.com

ISBN: 979-8-9960780-1-1

First Edition. Printed in the United States of America.

Important Notice — Legal Disclaimer

This book is written to give you practical, plain-language information about how car crash cases typically work. It is not legal advice and reading it does not make me — or anyone at Fair Squared Injury Law — your lawyer.

The law varies significantly from state to state. What applies in Colorado may not apply in your state. What applies to your neighbor's case may not apply to yours. Every car crash case is different, and only a licensed attorney in your state — who knows the specific facts of your situation — can give you actual legal advice.

No attorney-client relationship is created by reading this book, purchasing it, sharing it, or using it. The only way to form an attorney-client relationship with a licensed attorney is through a signed retainer or fee agreement.

Nothing in this book creates any warranty, express or implied, about the outcome of your case. The author has done his best to make this information accurate and useful, but makes no guarantees about results.

> **If your injuries are serious, if fault is disputed, if the insurance company is refusing to pay, or if you are on Medicare or Medicaid — stop reading and call a licensed personal injury attorney in your state right now. Some situations are too important to handle without professional legal help. If you are in Colorado or Wyoming, you can call our firm and schedule a free consultation: Fair Squared Injury Law, (720) 645-1123.**

That said — for the vast majority of straightforward car crash cases, the information in this book will genuinely help you. That is exactly why it was written.

Table of Contents

Introduction

Handling Your Own Car Crash Case

A car crash can upend your life in an instant. One moment you are driving to work, picking up your kids, or running an errand. The next moment everything stops — and suddenly you are dealing with injuries, a damaged vehicle, insurance companies, medical bills, and decisions you have never had to make before.

Most people have never navigated a car crash claim. The questions come fast: How do I pay for my medical care? Do I need a lawyer? What do I say to the insurance company? What if I say the wrong thing? What if I miss something important?

This book answers those questions. It walks you through every phase of a car crash case — from the scene of the crash through final settlement — in plain language you can actually use. You do not need a law degree to understand it. You just need to read it carefully and follow the steps.

■ Why Handle Your Own Case?

There are legitimate reasons to handle your own car crash case, and this book will help you do it well. The most common reasons people choose to go it alone include:

- Financial savings: Hiring an attorney typically means sharing a significant percentage of your settlement — sometimes up to 40% or more. If you handle the case yourself and reach a fair settlement, you keep more of the payout.
- Feasibility for smaller claims: For minor crashes with limited injuries — soft tissue soreness that resolves in a few weeks, no surgery, no hospitalization — hiring a lawyer may not be necessary or cost-effective.
- Speed: Sometimes your case can move from crash to settlement faster than if every step had to go through an attorney's office.

> **Handling your own case requires careful attention to detail, patience, and a commitment to following through. Even the simplest cases take months to finalize once your medical care is complete. Do not underestimate the time commitment.**

■ When You Absolutely Need a Lawyer

This book is honest with you about its limits. There are situations where handling your own case is not just difficult — it is a mistake that will cost you money. Here is when you need to stop and call an experienced personal injury trial attorney:

- Serious injuries: Broken bones, herniated spinal disks, surgeries, traumatic brain injuries, long-term disabilities, or any injury requiring advanced or ongoing medical treatment. These cases are too complex and too valuable to handle without legal representation.
- Disputed liability: If the other driver or their insurer disputes fault, or if multiple parties are involved, you need an attorney to investigate, gather evidence, and establish liability.
- Repeated lowball settlement offers: If the insurance company offers you only your medical bills plus a token amount for pain and suffering — $1,000, $2,000, or anything that does not reflect the real impact on your life — that is a lowball offer. An experienced trial attorney may be able to change that number.
- Legal proceedings: If your case goes to court, you need a lawyer. Full stop. What you see on TV bears almost no resemblance to actual litigation. The at-fault driver will have a lawyer paid for by their insurance company. You need one too.
- Medicare or Medicaid involvement: The rules around government program repayment are complex enough that attempting to navigate them alone is a serious mistake. Call an attorney first.
- Time: If you are recovering from significant injuries, managing a job and a family, and trying to handle a contested insurance claim at the same time — hiring an attorney reduces your involvement by 90% or more and eliminates most of the emotional strain.
- You were hit by a drunk or impaired driver: These cases carry the potential for punitive damages above and beyond your standard

injury compensation. Insurance companies know this and will work hard to minimize that exposure. You need an experienced trial attorney to make sure that potential is fully realized.

The person who caused your crash will have a lawyer defending them — paid for by their insurance company. That lawyer's job is to pay you as little as possible. If your case is serious, you need someone in your corner with equal firepower.

■ How This Book Is Organized

Each chapter covers a specific phase of the car crash case process, in the order you will actually encounter them:

- Chapter 1: What to do at the crash scene immediately after impact.
- Chapter 2: How to communicate with law enforcement and first responders.
- Chapter 3: Getting medical care — why timing matters and how to document everything.
- Chapter 4: Understanding your insurance coverage and how to contact each insurer.
- Chapter 5: Building your case with documentation — medical records, lost wages, and visual evidence.
- Chapter 6: Dealing with vehicle repairs, total loss determinations, and rental cars.
- Chapter 7: Communicating and negotiating with insurance adjusters.
- Chapter 8: Valuing your case beyond medical bills — pain, suffering, and human damages.
- Chapter 9: Finalizing your claim, writing your settlement letter, and managing your payout.
- Chapter 10: When to hire a lawyer and how to choose the right one.
- Chapter 11: Templates, checklists, and resources to help you stay organized.

At the back of the book you will find a sample settlement letter, a medical records request form, sample journal and log sheets, and a documentation checklist. These are the same tools we use at Fair Squared Injury Law. They work.

> **Read this entire book before you do anything else. The steps build on each other. Missing one step early can make every step that follows harder. The more prepared you are before you pick up the phone, the better your outcome will be.**

■ A Word About Time

Throughout this book you will hear me say it repeatedly: time is your enemy in a car crash case. Every day you wait to get medical care gives the insurance company ammunition to question whether you were really hurt. Every day you wait to set up your claim is a day the evidence gets colder. Every day you wait to act is a day closer to the statute of limitations — the legal deadline after which you can no longer sue.

> **TIME IS THE ENEMY. The steps in this book are time sensitive. Do not set this book down and come back to it in a week. Start now.**

With that said — Let's get to work.

Chapter 1

Immediate Actions at the Crash Scene

The moments immediately after a crash are chaotic, frightening, and critically important. What you do in those first minutes can protect your safety, preserve vital evidence, and set the foundation for everything that follows — your medical care, your insurance claim, and ultimately your settlement.

This chapter walks you through exactly what to do at the scene, in the order you should do it.

■ Safety First: Assess and Secure the Scene

Your safety and the safety of your passengers are your only priority in the immediate seconds after impact. Everything else comes second.

The first thing to do is assess your surroundings. Look for immediate hazards — oncoming traffic, fire, fuel leaks, or unstable vehicles. If you are on a busy road, staying in the roadway is one of the most dangerous places you can be. A second crash involving your stopped vehicle is a real and common danger.

> **SAFETY is your number one concern at the crash scene. Avoiding additional injury comes before documentation, before phone calls, before anything else.**

If you are able, take a few slow deep breaths before you act. Car crashes are traumatic and disorienting even for the most composed people. Nearly everyone reports feeling shook up or in shock in the minutes after a crash. That is completely normal. Slowing down for ten seconds to breathe will help you think more clearly.

■ Check on Your Passengers and Others Involved

Once you have assessed your own safety, check on your passengers. Keep them as calm as possible. If anyone is injured, do not attempt to physically move them unless leaving them in place will cause further harm — for example, if the vehicle is on fire.

Unless you are a trained medical professional or certified first responder, do not move anyone who cannot move themselves. Moving an injured person without proper training and equipment can cause serious injury or death. Wait for emergency services.

If it is safe to do so, approach the other vehicles involved and check on their occupants. Be cautious — other drivers may be disoriented, in pain, or emotionally distressed. Treat everyone calmly and with care.

■ Move Vehicles if It Is Safe to Do So

If your vehicle is drivable and it is safe to do so, move it off the road to a shoulder, parking lot, or other safe location. This reduces the risk of secondary crashes and protects everyone at the scene.

Police officers have a saying: “Crashes breed crashes.” It is remarkably common for additional collisions to occur at crash scenes because other drivers are distracted by the wreck or are not paying attention to stopped traffic ahead of them. Getting vehicles out of the active roadway protects you, other drivers, and the responding officers.

Some states require you to move your vehicle off the roadway if it is safe to do so. Others require you to leave it in place for investigative purposes. Know the law in your state. As a licensed driver, this is your responsibility.

If any vehicle has significant damage, is leaking fuel or other fluids, or if moving it would be unsafe for any reason — leave it where it is and wait for first responders.

■ Turn on Your Hazard Lights and Use Warning Devices

Turn on your hazard lights immediately. This alerts other drivers to the hazard ahead. Many newer vehicles activate hazard lights automatically after a crash — verify yours are on regardless.

If you have safety cones, flares, or reflective triangles in your vehicle and it is safe to deploy them, place them at least 50 feet behind the disabled vehicle to give approaching drivers advance warning.

> **Only deploy warning devices if you know how to use them and it is safe to do so. Do not put yourself in additional danger by walking into traffic to set out cones. Your safety always comes first.**

■ Call 911 — Every Time

Call 911 and report the crash. Do this on every crash, without exception.

I cannot count the number of times police were not called, and it turned out the at-fault driver had no license, no insurance, and was driving a car that was not theirs. Without a police report, you have no official record of what happened, who was involved, or what was observed at the scene. That official record is one of the most important pieces of evidence in your case.

> **Always call 911 after a crash. Always. The police report created at the scene is often the first document every insurance company will review when determining fault and processing your claim.**

Call 911 in all of the following situations:

- Any injuries, no matter how minor they appear
- Significant vehicle damage or airbag deployment

- Property damage such as damaged guardrails, utility boxes, or road signs
- Any situation where the law in your state requires it

■ How to Talk to the 911 Dispatcher

When the dispatcher answers, speak clearly and stay calm. Listen carefully — dispatchers are simultaneously collecting information from you and coordinating emergency response. Answer their questions directly.

Give them: the exact location of the crash including landmarks or cross streets, the number of vehicles involved, whether anyone appears injured, and any immediate hazards such as fuel leaks, fire, or blocked lanes.

Follow any instructions the dispatcher gives you. They are trained for exactly this situation. Their guidance keeps the scene safer while help is on the way.

■ What to Say — and What Not to Say — to the Police

When law enforcement arrives, keep your statements short, calm, and factual. Describe what happened in concrete terms without assigning blame or speculating about the other driver's actions or intentions.

Say: "I was traveling straight through the intersection on a green light and the other vehicle turned left in front of me."

Do not say: "The other driver wasn't paying attention" or "They must have been on their phone."

> **Stick to observable facts. Do not guess. Do not speculate. You were not inside the other driver's head and you do not know their intentions. Speculative**

> **statements create confusion and can be used against you later.**

I spent 22 years as a law enforcement officer before I became a trial lawyer. I am not anti-police. I have enormous respect for the work officers do. But I have also seen many people cause serious damage to their own cases by volunteering information to police that they were not required to give. Keep it factual. Keep it brief.

> **If the officer asks you to write down a statement, politely decline. In most states you are not required to provide a written statement to police. A written statement will be scrutinized by insurance companies later and can be used against you. Oral statements to police are documented in the report — that is sufficient.**

If you are asked about injuries, do not say you are fine or that you are not hurt. Adrenaline and shock mask pain. Serious injuries frequently do not manifest until hours or even days after a crash. Instead, describe exactly how you feel in that moment:

"I feel shaken up and disoriented. I'm going to get checked out by a doctor after I leave here."

That is the right answer. It is honest, it does not overstate, and it does not close the door on injuries that may emerge later.

■ Get the Crash Report Number and Officer Information

Before the responding officer leaves the scene, ask for the crash report number — sometimes called the case number. This number is how you obtain a copy of the official report later. Also ask for the officer's name, badge number, and contact information. Most officers carry business cards with space to write the case number.

> **Do not leave the scene without the crash report number. Without it, obtaining a copy of the police report later becomes significantly more difficult and time-consuming.**

■ Document the Scene Yourself

Do not rely on the police to document everything. Officers are managing a complex scene with multiple priorities. Your documentation is your responsibility.

If you are physically able and it is safe to do so, use your smartphone to photograph and video the scene thoroughly. Safety comes first — do not put yourself in danger to get photos.

Photos to take at minimum:

- All vehicles involved, from multiple angles, showing both overall damage and close-up details
- License plates of every vehicle involved
- The at-fault driver's license, insurance card, and vehicle registration — photograph these documents directly
- The surrounding area: road conditions, skid marks, debris, traffic signs, intersections, and weather conditions
- Your visible injuries, as soon as possible after the crash
- The inside of your vehicle, including any deployed airbags or damage to the interior

> **Modern smartphones automatically timestamp and geotag photos. This metadata is powerful evidence that verifies exactly when and where each photo was taken. Make sure your phone's location services are enabled.**

In addition to photos, record a video walkthrough of the scene if you can safely do so. Narrate as you go — "This is where my vehicle was struck," "These are the skid marks left by the at-fault vehicle." Video captures context and continuity that still photos sometimes miss.

> **I strongly recommend installing a dashcam in every vehicle you own. I had a client whose dashcam footage proved what actually happened at the scene — and prevented him from being wrongly charged with causing the crash. The footage also allowed him to pursue the correct at-fault driver's insurance company. A dashcam costs less than one hour of attorney time and can change everything.**

■ Collect Witness Information

Look around the scene for anyone who witnessed the crash — pedestrians, other drivers who stopped, people from nearby businesses. The police may collect witness information, but do not rely on them to do it. Collect it yourself.

Approach witnesses respectfully and ask for:

- Full name
- Phone number
- Email address and mailing address if they are willing to provide them
- A brief statement of what they saw — written down or recorded with their permission

> **Independent witnesses are among the most powerful evidence in a disputed liability case because they have no stake in the outcome and no reason to favor either side. Insurance companies and juries give significant weight to what neutral third parties saw. Get their information before they leave the scene.**

■ Exchange Information With the Other Driver

Exchange the following with every driver involved in the crash:

- Full name and contact information
- Driver's license number and state of issue
- Insurance company name and policy number
- Vehicle registration information

In most states, drivers are legally required to provide this information to other parties involved in a crash. If a driver refuses, note it for the police report and let the officer handle it.

> **Photograph the other driver's license, insurance card, and registration directly with your phone. Do not rely on writing down the information by hand — you may copy something incorrectly or miss a digit. A photo is exact and immediate.**

■ Write Down Your Personal Account as Soon as Possible

Memory fades fast after a traumatic event. As soon as you are safely away from the scene — that same day if possible — write down your own account of what happened. Include:

- The exact sequence of events leading up to the crash
- Weather and road conditions
- Traffic signal status if applicable
- Your vehicle's speed and position
- What you saw the other driver do

- What you heard and felt at the moment of impact
- Any statements made by the other driver at the scene

This personal record will help you recall accurate details weeks or months later when insurance companies start asking questions. It also helps your attorney if you eventually hire one.

> **The at-fault insurance company may dispute what happened and use that dispute as a basis for denying or reducing your claim. Good photographs, dashcam footage, witness information, and your personal written account shut that down immediately. Document everything.**

Chapter 2

Talking with Law Enforcement and First Responders

When law enforcement and first responders arrive at the scene, their presence is a stabilizing force. They secure the area, document what happened, and create the official record that every insurance company will rely on when determining fault. How you interact with them matters — not just for your safety, but for your case.

This chapter covers exactly what to say, what not to say, how to get the documentation you need, and what to do if the report contains errors.

▪ Stay Calm and Keep It Professional

Crashes are traumatic. Adrenaline is pumping, emotions are running high, and you may be in pain. All of that is understandable. But the single most important thing you can do when talking to law enforcement is stay calm and professional.

Think about it from the officer's perspective. They are arriving at a chaotic scene and trying to quickly determine what happened. Who are they more likely to listen to carefully and document accurately — the person who is composed and factual, or the person who is upset and talking over everyone?

> **Compose yourself before you speak. Take a breath. Be polite. A calm, professional demeanor makes your account more credible and your interaction with law enforcement more productive.**

Keep your statements brief and factual. This is not the time for a full narrative of everything you observed, felt, or believe about the other driver. Stick to what you know for certain and let the officer do their job.

▪ Describe Facts, Not Opinions

When describing what happened, speak only to what you directly observed. Describe your own actions and the sequence of events without attributing fault, guessing at the other driver's state of mind, or speculating about causes.

Say this: "I was traveling straight through the intersection on a green light. The other vehicle turned left in front of me and I had nowhere to go."

Not this: "The other driver wasn't paying attention" or "They must have been on their phone."

> **You were not inside the other driver's head. You do not know what they were thinking, what distracted them, or what caused them to act the way they did. Speculative statements create confusion in the report and give insurance companies ammunition to question your account. Stick to observable facts only.**

Avoid phrases like "I think," "maybe," "I'm guessing," or "I believe." These signal uncertainty and will be flagged by insurance adjusters reviewing the report. If you do not know something for certain, it is completely acceptable to say so: "I'm not sure" is a perfectly valid answer.

■ How to Describe Your Injuries to the Officer

This is one of the most important and most commonly mishandled parts of the scene interaction. Do not say you are fine. Do not say you are not hurt. Do not minimize what you are feeling in an attempt to seem tough or to avoid drama.

Adrenaline and shock are powerful. They mask pain. Serious injuries — herniated disks, torn ligaments, concussions, internal bleeding — frequently do not manifest until hours or even days after the crash. What feels like minor soreness at the scene can be a significant injury in the making.

> **Never tell the police you are not hurt. If the at-fault insurance company gets that report and sees you said you were fine at the scene, they will use it as their primary argument that you were not injured in the crash. Those words will follow your case all the way to settlement.**

The right answer when asked about injuries is to describe exactly how you feel in that moment, honestly and specifically:

"I feel shaken up and disoriented. My neck is sore. I'm going to see a doctor after I leave here."

That answer is honest. It does not overstate. It does not close the door on injuries that may develop later. And it documents the beginning of your medical trail.

Also tell the officer about any visible symptoms that might be overlooked: broken glasses, red marks or scrapes on your hands, arms, knees, or head, stiffness in your neck or back, dizziness, or nausea. These details belong in the report.

■ Do Not Provide a Written Statement at the Scene

An officer may ask you to write down your account of what happened. Politely decline.

In most states you are not legally required to provide a written statement to police at the crash scene. A written statement becomes a fixed, formal account that will be scrutinized word by word by insurance companies. If any detail in that statement later proves incomplete or inconsistent with new information — injuries that developed over the following days, witness accounts, dashcam footage — the insurance company will use that inconsistency against you.

> **Politely decline any request for a written statement at the scene. If the officer insists, tell them you want to consult with an attorney before putting anything in**

> **writing. The police cannot compel you to write a statement. Your oral account to the responding officer will be documented in the report — that is sufficient.**

I spent 22 years as a law enforcement officer. I have deep respect for the work police do. I am not telling you to be uncooperative — I am telling you to be smart. There is a significant difference between cooperating with law enforcement and volunteering written documentation that can be used against you months later by an insurance company.

■ Get the Crash Report Number and Officer Information

Before the officer leaves the scene, make sure you have two things: the crash report number and the officer's contact information.

The crash report number — sometimes called the case number — is how you obtain a copy of the official report. Without it, tracking down your report later becomes unnecessarily difficult and time-consuming. Most officers carry business cards and can write the case number directly on the card for you.

Also get the officer's name, badge number, and department contact information. You may need to follow up if the report contains errors, if you have questions about what was documented, or if the insurance company needs to verify details directly with the responding officer.

> **Do not leave the scene without the crash report number. Write it down. Photograph it. Put it somewhere you will not lose it. This number is the key to your official crash record.**

■ How to Obtain a Copy of the Crash Report

Most crash reports are available within three to ten business days of the crash, though processing times vary significantly from one police agency to another. Before making a trip to the records department, call ahead to confirm the report is ready and to ask what payment methods are accepted.

Many police agencies now offer online portals where you can request and download the report for a small fee. This is often the fastest and most convenient option. Check the agency's website first.

Fees for crash reports typically range from $10 to $20, but we have seen agencies charge $100 or more when the request includes the full report, scene photographs, and officer body camera footage. Know the cost before you go and bring the right payment method — many departments only accept credit cards, debit cards with a PIN, or cash.

> **Get the crash report as soon as it is available. The sooner you have it, the sooner you can identify any errors and address them. Insurance companies will be reviewing this report too — you want to know what it says before they do.**

■ Review the Report Carefully for Errors

Once you have a copy of the crash report, read every line carefully. Common errors include:

- Incorrect vehicle descriptions — wrong make, model, color, or year
- Misspelled names for drivers, passengers, or witnesses
- Missing passenger names
- Incorrect statements attributed to you
- Incomplete or inaccurate descriptions of what happened
- Wrong license plate numbers

Reports often contain coded boxes in the margins. You can search online for the specific agency's crash report code key to decode them. These codes frequently contain information about posted speed limits, estimated vehicle speeds at the time of impact, and the officer's preliminary determination of fault.

> **If you obtained the officer's body camera footage, review it alongside the written report. The footage can help you identify discrepancies between what was actually said at the scene and what ended up in the written record. It can also help you recover correct names, license plate numbers, and other details that may have been transcribed incorrectly.**

If you find errors, contact the responding officer directly by email or phone to request a correction. Document that you made this request. Many officers will decline to amend a completed report — some departments have strict policies against it. If that happens, note the discrepancies in your own records and be prepared to address them when dealing with the insurance companies.

■ Requesting an Amendment to the Report

If there is a significant factual error in the crash report — a wrong name, an incorrect license plate number, a misattributed statement — you can formally request an amendment through the agency's records department.

Contact the records department, explain the specific error, and ask about their amendment process. Some departments allow minor corrections with supporting documentation. Others require a more formal process. Some will not allow citizen-initiated amendments at all unless you can provide overwhelming evidence that the report is factually wrong.

> **Not every error in a crash report can be corrected. What matters is that you document the discrepancy in your own records and raise it directly with the**

insurance companies when it becomes relevant. Your photographs, dashcam footage, and witness accounts are independent evidence that can counter an inaccurate report.

■ The Crash Report Is the Foundation of Your Claim

The crash report is almost always the first document every insurance company reviews when determining fault and processing claims. It carries the weight of a professional law enforcement assessment of the scene. Accurate details, witness statements, and fault determinations documented in that report will either support your claim or create headwinds against it.

This is why everything in this chapter matters. Being calm and factual at the scene produces a better report. Getting the report number before you leave ensures you can obtain it quickly. Reviewing it carefully for errors means you catch problems before the insurance company does.

<u>TIME IS THE ENEMY</u>.

The sooner you have a copy of the crash report, the sooner you can identify any issues that need to be addressed. Do not wait weeks to request it. Call the records department within a few days of the crash and find out when it will be ready.

Your attention to detail at this stage sets the foundation for every step that follows.

Chapter 3

Seeking Medical Care

Obtaining medical care should be one of your top priorities after a car crash.

> **<u>TIME IS THE ENEMY</u>. Waiting even a day to obtain post-crash medical care can permanently damage your case. Waiting a week will make it nearly impossible for you to handle your case yourself.**

I cannot stress this enough: **GET CHECKED BY A MEDICAL DOCTOR AS SOON AS YOU LEAVE THE CRASH SCENE.**

Timely and appropriate medical attention is not only essential for your health — it is critical for supporting any claim you might need to make for injury compensation. One of the biggest objections I hear from insurance companies when trying to settle cases is how long the person waited to get post-crash medical care. They use every day of delay as ammunition against you.

■ Hidden Injuries and Delayed Pain

Car crashes trigger a rush of adrenaline and shock that can completely mask the symptoms of serious injuries. Even if you feel fine at the scene, underlying injuries like whiplash, internal bleeding, or a concussion can develop hours or even days later. Go to the emergency room. An ER doctor is trained to fully evaluate trauma injuries and identify what your body is not yet telling you.

Here is an extreme but real example from my own practice.

I had a client whose neck was "really sore" for two days after a rear-end crash. The car was damaged but still drivable, so he drove himself home. Two days later, when the pain would not go away, he finally went to the ER. The diagnosis: a broken neck. He could have died. He could have been paralyzed. He walked around for two days with a broken neck because the adrenaline and shock of the crash told him he was fine.

Do not let this happen to you. Go to the ER after a car crash. Your health is worth more than the cost of the visit.

Here is my own example.

I was stopped at a red light when a driver high on drugs rear-ended my car. The impact crunched my car but did not deploy the airbags. My lower back hurt right away, but it was not debilitating — I thought it was just soreness. I went to the ER immediately and was told I had sprains and strains in my back, shoulder, and neck. Two days later, when I saw my own doctor, my back pain had gotten significantly worse. An MRI revealed a herniated and ruptured spinal disk in my lower back. I will live with that injury for the rest of my life.

I am a personal injury attorney who has handled hundreds of crash cases. I went to the ER immediately. I still ended up with a permanent injury I did not fully understand until days later. If it can happen to me, it can happen to you.

If you are diagnosed with a new disk injury after a crash, you need a lawyer. Insurance companies will not pay full value on a disk injury case without one.

■ Early Care Prevents Long-Term Problems

Early medical evaluation does more than document your injuries — it prevents them from getting worse. Untreated spinal injuries lead to chronic pain and mobility issues that worsen over time. Head injuries, including concussions and traumatic brain injuries, can have severe long-term consequences if not addressed promptly. Closed head injuries are more common in car crashes than most people realize, and their effects can last months, years, or longer.

A medical doctor is the only person qualified to evaluate, treat, and refer you appropriately for these injuries. A chiropractor cannot credibly diagnose a concussion as far as an insurance company is concerned. Start with a medical doctor.

▪ What to Expect at the Emergency Room or Urgent Care

When you arrive at the ER or urgent care, the medical team will perform a standard trauma evaluation. This typically includes checking your vital signs, conducting a physical examination, and ordering X-rays or other imaging to identify injured body parts. Their primary goal is to rule out hidden life-threatening injuries first.

When you describe your symptoms, be as thorough and specific as possible. Tell the doctor and nursing staff about every area of pain, dizziness, discomfort, or unusual sensation — even if it seems minor. Do not minimize or downplay anything. What feels like minor soreness at the scene can be documented evidence of injury that matters enormously later.

> **Be honest about any pre-existing injuries. If your left back hurt before the crash and now your right back hurts, say so clearly. A previous injury does not disqualify you from compensation for new crash-caused injuries — but the record needs to distinguish between the two.**

Before you leave the facility, ask how to obtain a complete copy of your medical records — not just the discharge summary. You want all notes, imaging studies, lab work, and medications given or prescribed. This full record is essential for your case. The discharge summary alone is not sufficient.

▪ Follow-Up Care: Why Every Appointment Matters

After your initial ER or urgent care visit, schedule your follow-up appointments immediately and attend every single one. Follow-up care is critically important if you develop new symptoms or if your pain worsens after the initial visit.

> **Missing medical appointments is one of the most damaging things you can do to your case. Insurance companies treat missed appointments as evidence that you "must not be that hurt." Do not give them that weapon.**

Yes, it can feel tiresome. Yes, you may have days where you wonder if the treatment is helping. Go anyway. Document every visit. Follow every care plan. The paper trail you build through consistent treatment is one of the most powerful tools you have when it comes time to negotiate your settlement.

If you develop new symptoms or your existing pain worsens at any point during your treatment, contact your doctor immediately. Do not wait for your next scheduled appointment.

■ The Six-Week Rule: When Conservative Care Is Not Enough

> **If your crash-related pain has not started to improve after six weeks of treatment, stop and reassess. Request imaging — most likely an MRI — from the doctor overseeing your care. Do not wait for them to suggest it. Ask for it directly.**

Most minor soft tissue injuries begin to heal within four to six weeks of consistent treatment. If you are still at the same pain level after six weeks of chiropractic care or physical therapy, something else is going on. Extended conservative care without identifying a specific diagnosis — a herniated disk, narrowing of spinal spacing (stenosis), or a torn ligament — does two things: it fails to get you the treatment you actually need, and it gives insurance companies ammunition to question whether you were seriously injured at all.

Advocate for yourself. If your doctor will not order imaging after six weeks of no improvement, get a second opinion from a doctor who specializes in crash injuries. You are not being difficult. You are doing exactly what you should do.

■ Types of Healthcare Providers and When to Use Them

After your initial ER or urgent care evaluation, your follow-up care will likely involve several types of providers. Here is what each one does and how they fit into your case.

■ Primary Care Physicians (M.D., D.O., or Physiatrist)

A primary care physician provides overall oversight of your recovery, evaluates the need for specialist referrals, and monitors symptoms that develop over time. Having a medical doctor actively directing your care adds significant credibility to your case. Insurance companies regard MDs as objective authorities on injury — a treatment plan directed by an MD carries far more weight than one directed solely by a chiropractor or physical therapist.

Your primary care doctor can also order imaging tests — MRIs, CT scans, X-rays — to identify injuries not visible through a physical exam alone. These scans are essential for diagnosing spinal disk injuries, ligament tears, joint injuries, and fractures. Even if you had imaging done at the ER, your treating physician will often need updated imaging to properly monitor your recovery and direct your long-term care.

> **Many people are surprised to learn they suffered shoulder injuries in a rear-end crash. It is more common than you think. If your shoulder hurts after a crash, tell your doctor and ask whether imaging is appropriate.**

■ Chiropractors

Chiropractors specialize in musculoskeletal issues, particularly spinal alignment and soft tissue injuries. For injuries like recurring headaches, whiplash, neck pain, or back pain, chiropractic care can be effective in managing pain and supporting recovery.

However, chiropractic care should always be directed by a medical doctor, not the other way around. See an M.D. first to rule out more serious conditions before starting chiropractic treatment. Insurance companies are deeply suspicious of cases where chiropractic care is the only treatment — they regularly use "chiropractic-only" treatment as a basis for arguing your injuries were not serious, even when they were.

> **More than 18 chiropractic visits without a specific documented diagnosis is a red flag to insurance adjusters. If your chiropractor cannot point to a specific pain generator — a herniated disk, narrowing of spinal spacing (stenosis), or a torn ligament — the insurance company will use that gap against you.**

■ Physical Therapists

Physical therapists help restore mobility and strength after an injury through targeted exercises and rehabilitation techniques. Physical therapy is especially valuable for soft tissue injuries, joint damage, and improving range of motion. It is common for your medical doctor to refer you to both chiropractic care and physical therapy in the six to eight weeks following your crash.

Work with your physical therapist to establish a structured treatment plan that includes both in-office sessions and a Home Exercise Plan (HEP) — exercises you perform on your own between appointments. This documentation shows you are actively working toward recovery and following professional medical guidance. It also supports your case by demonstrating that you pursued the least invasive and least expensive treatment options first — which makes it harder for the insurance company to devalue your case when your doctor begins recommending more advanced care.

■ Orthopedic Surgeons and Neurologists

If you experience persistent pain, numbness, tingling, burning, or shooting pain after your crash, you may need to see an orthopedic surgeon or neurologist. These specialists diagnose and treat injuries to bones, joints, the brain, and the nervous system. What people commonly describe as a "pinched nerve" is often an injury to bone or connective tissue pressing on nerve pathways — an orthopedic surgeon or neurologist is the right provider to evaluate and treat this.

> **Even a "minor" concussion warrants neurological evaluation. Concussions are cumulative — a second concussion compounding an unresolved first one can have lasting consequences. Do not dismiss a head injury because it seems mild. See a neurologist.**

■ Pain Management Specialists

Chronic pain — pain that persists beyond a few weeks or months and does not respond to conservative care — may require a pain management specialist. These doctors go beyond chiropractic, massage, and physical therapy to offer injections, medications, and advanced treatments such as stem cell therapy and platelet-rich plasma (PRP) therapy to address damaged tissues and potentially help you avoid or delay surgery.

> **If you find yourself needing advanced pain management treatments, get a lawyer on your case immediately. Insurance companies will fight hard to avoid paying for these expensive therapies. You need an advocate.**

■ When to Get a Second Opinion

If your recovery feels stagnant — if your pain levels have plateaued after a couple of months and your doctor is not recommending next steps — ask directly about advanced imaging or a specialist referral. If you do not get a satisfactory answer, seek a second opinion.

Look for providers experienced in treating car crash or slip-and-fall injuries. Orthopedic surgeons, neurologists, pain management doctors, and physiatrists are all appropriate sources for a second opinion. Check your health insurance network for specialists in these areas. If you do not have health insurance, a personal injury attorney can often connect you with doctors who work with crash injury patients.

Having more than one qualified medical provider document your injuries and their cause makes it significantly harder for the insurance company to discount or marginalize your claim. Every additional medical perspective that confirms your injuries is another layer of evidence they have to overcome.

■ Documenting Your Medical Treatment

Thorough documentation of your injuries and treatment is the foundation of your case. Every medical record is evidence — evidence of what happened to your body, how it has affected your life, and what it has cost you. Here is how to do it right.

■ Collecting Your Records

Gather all relevant records from every provider who treated you: discharge summaries, imaging results (X-rays, MRIs, CT scans), doctor's notes, prescriptions, and specialist referral notes. If you were prescribed physical therapy, chiropractic care, massage therapy, or any other specialist treatment, request records from each of those providers as well.

When requesting billing records, ask specifically for itemized billing statements that include the billing and treatment codes for each service. The bills mailed to your home are not sufficient — they do not include the codes the insurance company needs to process your claim. Also save all pharmacy receipts for crash-related prescriptions, or ask your pharmacy for a summary of relevant medications filled.

■ Organizing Your Records

Set up a dedicated file — digital or paper — for all crash-related medical records, bills, receipts, and notes. Organize everything chronologically starting with your ER or urgent care visit. You will need electronic versions of your documents to submit to the insurance company. Sending paper is not advised.

Consider maintaining a log or spreadsheet tracking each medical appointment, procedure, test, and associated cost. Search online for "medical log sheet" or "medical chronology example" for a useful template. This log becomes a quick reference when you are building your settlement demand.

▪ Separating Crash-Related Care From Unrelated Care

When reviewing your records, clearly separate treatments related to the crash from any unrelated health issues. Insurers only reimburse for crash-caused injuries. Submitting unrelated records — immunizations, a flu visit, treatment for an unrelated condition — does not help you. It confuses your claim, gives the insurance company excuses to delay payment, and invites them to dig into your medical history for ways to devalue your case.

> **You are not required to give the at-fault insurance company records unrelated to your crash injuries. You are also not required to sign a medical release allowing them to pull your records themselves. The only exception is your own insurance company when accessing uninsured motorist, underinsured motorist, or medical payments (PIP) coverage. If you are unsure, refuse the release and call a lawyer before signing anything.**

▪ Working With Your Health Insurance

Notify your health insurance provider that you were in a car crash. Even if you do not notify them proactively, they will find out — the billing codes on your medical records will tell them. Some insurers require notification to avoid complications with your claim later. Provide proof of the crash when asked.

Be aware that in some states, including Colorado, it is illegal for a health insurance company to refuse coverage for crash-caused medical expenses. If your health insurer refuses to pay your crash-related bills, contact a personal injury attorney. Your co-pays and deductibles will still apply, but the underlying bills cannot lawfully be denied in states with this protection.

■ Understanding Subrogation

Subrogation is the process by which your health insurance carrier gets reimbursed for the money they spent on your crash-caused medical care once you receive a settlement from the at-fault party's insurance. Understand your health plan's subrogation policy before you settle so there are no surprises at the end of your case.

If you are on Medicare, hire a personal injury attorney before you go any further.

Medicare has strict rules on repayment and on setting aside funds for future crash-related care. Failure to comply can result in denial of your Medicare benefits. This is an area which requires expert advice and is not an area to navigate alone.

Chapter 4

Understanding Insurance and Coverage Options

Understanding insurance coverage is vital when handling your own car crash case. Knowing what types of coverage apply, how to report the crash, and how to navigate insurance policies will help you avoid common pitfalls and ensure you obtain full value for your case.

This chapter also incorporates two steps that must happen immediately after the crash: notifying your health insurance carrier in writing, and notifying both insurance companies of your vehicle's location. These are among the most commonly overlooked steps in the entire process.

■ The "Full Coverage" Myth

> **"Full coverage" is one of the most misleading terms in the insurance industry. It does not cover everything. In fact, it does not cover your injuries at all.**

When someone buys "full coverage," they have purchased Liability, Comprehensive, and Collision coverage — and nothing else. The additional coverages that actually protect you after a crash are separate purchases that most people never make.

"Full coverage" includes: Liability, Comprehensive, and Collision.

"Full coverage" does <u>NOT</u> include: Uninsured/Underinsured Motorist coverage, Medical Payments/PIP coverage, Towing benefits, or Rental Car coverage if your car is not drivable.

> **Full coverage does not pay for your medical care after a crash. It does not pay your hospital bills, your chiropractor, or your physical therapist. If you want coverage for your own injuries, you must buy it separately.**

■ Types of Coverage: What Each One Does and Why It Matters

■ 1. Liability Insurance

Liability insurance is required in most states and covers damages and injuries that you cause to other drivers, passengers, pedestrians, or property. It does not cover your own vehicle or your own medical expenses.

Liability insurance has two components:

- Bodily Injury Liability ("BI"): Covers medical expenses, lost wages, and non-economic damages for people you injure. Most BI policies also include coverage for an attorney to defend you if you are sued. States mandate minimum coverage levels.
- Property Damage Liability ("PD"): Pays for repairs or replacement of another person's vehicle or property that you damaged.

Liability policies have limits — a maximum payout per person injured, per accident, and for property damage. A common minimum policy might offer $25,000 per person, $50,000 per accident, and $15,000 in property damage. In most crashes, these minimum amounts are woefully inadequate.

> **Even the cheapest new cars cost more than the minimum property damage coverage in most states. An ER visit after a crash regularly runs into five figures. If you own a home or have investments, your liability coverage should equal or exceed the value of those assets. Minimum coverage is not for homeowners or those with assets.**

Do not make the mistake of buying the cheapest policy available. In some cases, even filing for bankruptcy will not discharge damages caused by a car crash. They can follow you for the rest of your life. Consult a trusted insurance expert and an attorney before making coverage decisions.

■ 2. Comprehensive and Collision Insurance

Comprehensive coverage pays for damage to your vehicle caused by objects other than other vehicles — hail, animals, falling trees. Collision coverage pays for damage caused by hitting another vehicle or object. Together, these make up what most people call "full coverage" for their vehicle.

Both come with a deductible — the amount you pay out of pocket before insurance covers the rest. If your deductible is $1,000 and your repair costs $5,000, you pay $1,000 and insurance covers $4,000.

> **Keep your deductible at or below what you currently have in your bank account — and never more than $500. A deductible you cannot pay immediately means a car you cannot get repaired.**

Many people hesitate to use their own collision insurance when the other driver is at fault, fearing a rate increase. This fear is generally unfounded. If you were not at fault, your insurer will pursue reimbursement from the at-fault insurer through subrogation. In most states, including Colorado, your rates cannot be increased for a crash you did not cause. Using your own insurance is almost always faster than waiting for the at-fault insurer to accept liability.

■ 3. Uninsured/Underinsured Motorist Coverage (UM/UIM)

Uninsured Motorist (UM) coverage pays for your bodily injuries if the at-fault driver has no insurance. Underinsured Motorist (UIM) coverage pays when the at-fault driver's policy limits are not enough to cover your damages. Both cover medical expenses, lost wages, pain and suffering, and other non-economic damages. We refer to them as UM/UIM throughout the book.

UM/UIM does not pay for damage to your vehicle. It covers your body, not your car. This is a separate coverage from collision and is not part of "full coverage."

Few states require UM/UIM coverage. Most make it optional. Buy it anyway. The roads are full of drivers carrying minimum or no insurance. UM/UIM coverage is one of the most important protections you can purchase for yourself and your family.

■ 4. Medical Payments (MedPay) / Personal Injury Protection (PIP)

MedPay and PIP coverage pay your medical expenses after a crash regardless of who was at fault. They can reimburse out-of-pocket costs like prescription co-pays, braces, and deductibles. Some PIP policies also cover lost wages and rehabilitation costs.

- PIP: Broader coverage. Required in "no-fault" states. May cover lost wages, household services, and more. If you are in a no-fault state, contact a local attorney to understand your rights before proceeding with any claim.
- MedPay: Covers medical expenses only. More common in fault-based states. Optional in most states.

We recommend our clients carry the highest level of MedPay coverage available in their state. It provides fast payment for covered medical expenses, protects your credit from collection actions during the time your case is pending, and reduces the financial stress of treatment. It is not part of "full coverage" — you must buy it separately.

MedPay and PIP generally do not apply to motorcycle or off-road vehicle crashes. Specialty policies are required for those vehicles.

■ First Steps After the Crash: Notify Both Insurers of Your Vehicle's Location

Before you do anything else regarding your vehicle, call both the at-fault insurance company AND your own insurance company and give each of them the exact location of your car — the address of the tow yard, storage facility, or wherever it currently sits.

> **Storage fees at tow yards and auto storage facilities can reach $75 to $150 per day or more. These fees accumulate fast. Notifying both carriers immediately eliminates their ability to later claim they did not know where the vehicle was and use that as an excuse to deny or reduce payment of storage costs.**

The at-fault insurance company is responsible for your storage fees — but only if they know where the car is and have the opportunity to move it to one of their own free or reduced-cost storage facilities. Your own insurance company needs the same information so they can coordinate on your behalf.

Make both calls the same day as the crash if possible, or first thing the following morning. Get the name of the person you spoke with and note the date and time of each call. No knowledge = no excuse. Give them both the information and document that you did.

■ Contacting Your Own Insurance Company

Call your insurance company as soon as possible after the crash and set up a claim. Have the following ready:

- Date, time, and location of the crash
- Weather and visibility conditions
- Police report number, if available

- License plate numbers and contact information for other drivers involved
- A brief factual description of what happened

Provide photos, witness information, and your ER or urgent care discharge summary if you have it. Let your insurer know you have this documentation.

> **Your own insurance policies — collision, UM/UIM, and MedPay/PIP — are contracts between you and your insurer. You have a duty to cooperate. Give them recorded statements and sign medical releases when asked. Failure to cooperate can give your insurer grounds to deny your claim.**

When giving a recorded statement to your own insurer, be honest but be careful. It is completely acceptable to say "I don't know" or "I'm not sure" when those are the true answers. Do not guess about fault or about the full extent of your injuries — you may not know the full picture yet. Stick to what you know for certain.

> **Tell your own insurance company they are not authorized to share any information with the at-fault insurance company — even if both you and the at-fault driver are insured by the same company. State this clearly and in writing.**

■ Contacting the At-Fault Driver's Insurance Company

The at-fault driver's insurance is fundamentally different from your own. This is "3rd Party" coverage — the BI and PD policies that cover damage and injuries the at-fault driver caused. This insurer has no contract with you and no obligation to look out for your interests. Their job is to protect their insured and minimize what they pay you.

When setting up your claim, give them the basic information: crash location, date, police report number, and vehicle descriptions. Do not go further than that in your initial call.

Do NOT agree to a recorded statement with the at-fault insurance company. This is very likely to be used against you. Adjusters will sometimes tell you they cannot determine fault without your statement. This is almost never true — they can get fault information from the police report and from their own insured driver.

Here is how this plays out in real life: the day after the crash you give a recorded statement saying you are "just a little sore." Three days later your pain has dramatically worsened and an MRI reveals a herniated disk. When you try to settle, the adjuster pulls out your recorded statement and reminds you that you said you were barely hurt. Do not give them that weapon.

Do NOT sign any documents or medical releases from the at-fault insurance company at this stage. They may try to obtain your full medical history. They are not entitled to it. They are entitled to records related to your crash-caused injuries — nothing more.

■ One Thing You Are Required to Disclose to the At-Fault Insurer

While you are generally not required to give the at-fault insurance company a recorded statement or sign medical releases, there is one piece of information you are legally required to disclose: whether or not you are on Medicare.

Tell them. Federal law requires all parties in a personal injury settlement to notify Medicare when a Medicare beneficiary is involved. Insurance companies are required to report settlements to Medicare regardless of whether you tell them or not. Attempting to hide your Medicare status or work around Medicare's repayment rights can result in denial of your future Medicare benefits and legal action against you for repayment — plus interest and penalties.

If you are on Medicare, stop and call a personal injury attorney before you go any further. Medicare's rules around repayment and future medical set-asides are too complex to navigate alone.

■ Notifying Your Health Insurance Carrier

One step that people almost always overlook is notifying their health insurance carrier in writing that they were involved in a car crash and are using their health insurance for crash-related medical care. This notification protects you and preserves your right to have your health insurance pay your medical bills while your case is pending.

Your notification letter must include all of the following:

- Your full legal name
- Your health insurance member ID number
- The name of the primary insured on the health plan, if that is not you
- The date of the crash
- A brief description of which body parts were injured
- Your mailing address, email address, and phone number

Mail this letter to the address on your health insurance card, or call the member services number on the back of your card to get the correct address for crash-related notifications. Keep a copy of the letter and your proof of mailing.

Even if you do not notify your health insurer proactively, they will find out — the billing codes on your medical records will tell them. Some insurers require notification to avoid claim complications. Notify them in writing anyway. It protects you.

Most health insurance carriers are entitled to be paid back — through subrogation — for the money they spent on your crash-caused medical care. You will need to determine the exact amount owed at the end of your case before you finalize any settlement.

In some states, including Colorado, it is illegal for a health insurance company to refuse to cover crash-caused medical expenses. If your health insurer refuses to pay your crash-related bills, contact a personal injury attorney immediately.

> **If you are on Medicare or Medicaid, these government programs MUST be repaid from your settlement. There are no exceptions. Failing to repay them can result in denial of your future benefits and legal action to recover the money — with interest and penalties added on top. If you are on Medicare or Medicaid, hire a personal injury attorney to handle your case.**

■ Disclosing Policy Limits: What You Are Entitled to Know

Policy limits determine the maximum payout available from each insurance policy. Understanding the at-fault driver's limits early helps you make informed decisions about whether their coverage is sufficient or whether you will need to rely on your own UM/UIM coverage.

Some states, including Colorado, require insurers to disclose policy limits upon request. There are specific procedures and forms involved. Do an internet search for your state's auto insurance policy limit disclosure requirements, or call a local personal injury attorney — most will answer this question for free.

If the at-fault insurance company will not tell you their policy limits directly, use this exact phrasing:

> ***"Is this a state minimum policy?"***

This forces a yes or no answer. If yes — you now know the minimum coverage amounts for your state. If no — you know there is more coverage available and you can press further.

> **Never guess at the policy limits and never accept a settlement without knowing what they are. Settling for less than the policy limits when you are entitled to more is one of the most common and most costly mistakes people make when handling their own case.**

■ Document Every Communication With Every Insurer

From the moment you set up your claims, keep a written log of every interaction with every insurance company. For each contact, note:

- Date and time of the call or email
- Name of the person you spoke with
- Company and department they work for
- Summary of what was said and what was agreed to

Use email whenever possible. Email creates a written record that cannot be disputed later. Save every piece of correspondence — every letter, every email, every text — from every insurer involved in your case.

> **Insurance companies will sometimes tell you they said or did something that never happened. A good communication log shuts that down immediately. If you eventually hire an attorney, this log also means they will not have to repeat tasks you have already completed — saving time and money on your case.**

■ Redacting Medical Records Before Sending to Insurance Companies

Redacting means blacking out or removing items from a document that are not relevant to your claim. When you submit medical records to the at-fault insurance company, you are only required to provide records related to your crash-caused injuries. Everything else is private.

Examples of items to redact before submitting records to the at-fault insurer:

- Family medical history
- Social history unrelated to the crash
- Conditions having nothing to do with the crash, such as asthma or diabetes
- Treatment for body parts not injured in the crash — for example, a previous left arm surgery when only your back and right shoulder were injured

> **Do not use a black marker to cover sensitive items. A marker can be scanned through. Use a secure PDF redaction tool such as Adobe Acrobat. Verify that the redacted information is permanently removed and cannot be recovered before sending.**

Do not be surprised if the at-fault insurer claims they cannot process your claim without your complete unredacted records. This is almost never true. Contact a personal injury attorney in your state if they threaten to deny your claim based on incomplete records.

> **You are not required to give the at-fault insurance company records unrelated to your crash injuries. You are also not required to sign a blanket medical release allowing them to pull your records themselves. Refuse the release and call a lawyer before signing anything you are unsure about.**

■ Understanding Subrogation: Paying Back What Was Spent on Your Behalf

Subrogation is the legal process by which an insurance company that paid your bills gets reimbursed from your settlement. This applies to health insurance, MedPay, and government programs like Medicaid and Medicare.

Familiarize yourself with your health plan's subrogation policy before you settle. At the end of your case, you will need to contact each insurer or program that paid on your behalf and obtain a final payback amount in writing before you finalize your settlement.

> **Repaying Medicare and Medicaid for money they spent on your crash caused medical care are not optional.**
>
> **These programs WILL find out about your settlement because all insurance companies are required by law to notify them — even if you are not currently receiving those benefits.**
>
> **Failing to repay these government programs can result in denial of future benefits and legal action against you for the full amount owed, plus interest and possibly attorney's fees.**

Most personal injury attorneys will handle Medicare and Medicaid subrogation as part of representing you. They generally will not handle only the subrogation portion of a case because they will not have the full case information needed to properly navigate the repayment amounts. If you are on Medicare or Medicaid, the safest and most practical path is to hire a personal injury attorney.

Chapter 5

Building Your Case with Documentation

Documentation is the backbone of your case. A picture is worth a thousand words, and a complete, organized, chronological file of your medical records, billing, lost wages, and visual evidence is worth thousands of dollars at the negotiating table.

The insurance company will scrutinize everything you submit. If your documentation is incomplete, disorganized, or includes irrelevant material, they will use that against you. If it is thorough, chronological, and precisely targeted to your crash-caused injuries and losses, it becomes very difficult for them to dispute the value of your claim.

This chapter walks you through exactly what to collect, how to organize it, and how to present it effectively.

■ Your Right to Free Medical Records

Before we get into organization, know this: you are legally entitled to your medical records. Under the 21st Century Cures Act, patients have the right to access their health information at minimal or no cost. Many healthcare providers are required to provide you with one free electronic copy of your records annually.

To obtain your records, contact each provider's records department and complete their release form, which is often available on their website. Always request an electronic copy first — it is usually free, immediately usable, and easier to organize and send to insurance companies. Physical copies may carry a per-page printing fee.

> **Your medical providers are required by law to provide you with a complete copy of your medical billing and records upon your written request. Do not let any provider tell you otherwise. In many cases you can pick up your billing ledger and records the same day you request them.**

■ Medical Records: What to Collect

Gather records from every provider who treated you for crash-caused injuries. This includes:

- Emergency room visit records, including all doctor's notes, nursing notes, imaging studies, lab work, and discharge summaries
- Urgent care records if you were seen there instead of or in addition to the ER
- Primary care physician records for all crash-related visits
- Specialist records — orthopedic surgeons, neurologists, pain management doctors, physiatrists
- Chiropractic records
- Physical therapy records
- Mental health records if you sought treatment for crash-caused psychological impacts
- Prescription records for all crash-related medications

> **The bills mailed to your home are not sufficient. They do not contain the treatment and billing codes the insurance company needs to process your claim. You must order a complete itemized billing ledger from each provider. For an ER visit, this typically means three separate billing requests: the hospital bill, the treating physicians' bill, and the radiologist's bill.**

Request itemized billing statements specifically — not just the summary bill. An itemized statement lists every charge by treatment, procedure, and billing code. This is the document the insurance company requires to evaluate and pay your medical claims.

Also save every pharmacy receipt for crash-related prescriptions. If you did not save them, ask your pharmacy for a complete summary of all relevant medications filled since the date of the crash.

■ How to Organize Your Medical File

Once you have collected your records and bills, organize everything chronologically — starting from the day of the crash and progressing through your last day of treatment.

The recommended order for each provider visit is: medical records first, then the corresponding billing for that visit. Start with your ER records, followed by the ER billing. Then your first follow-up visit records, then that billing. Continue this pattern through every provider and every visit through the end of your treatment.

> **This chronological structure tells a clear story: here is what happened to my body, here is how it was treated, here is what it cost, from the day of the crash to the day I finished treatment. That narrative makes it significantly harder for an insurance company to dispute the connection between the crash and your injuries.**

Maintain your file digitally. Insurance companies prefer electronic submissions and paper documents slow the process down. Create a master folder with clearly labeled subfolders for each provider, and a separate folder for billing.

Also maintain a log or spreadsheet tracking each medical appointment, the provider seen, the diagnosis or treatment, and the associated cost. An internet search for "medical log sheet" or "medical chronology example" will give you a useful template. This log becomes your quick reference when building your settlement demand.

■ Redacting Medical Records Before Submission

When you submit medical records to the at-fault insurance company, you are only required to provide records related to your crash-caused injuries. Everything else is private and should be removed before you send anything.

Redacting means permanently blocking out or removing content from a document. Items to redact before submitting records to the at-fault insurer include:

- Family medical history
- Social history unrelated to the crash
- Conditions with no connection to the crash — such as asthma, diabetes, or prior surgeries on body parts not injured in the crash
- Treatment records for visits unrelated to the crash — a flu visit, an annual physical, immunizations
- Mental health history unrelated to crash-caused psychological impacts

Use a proper PDF redaction tool such as Adobe Acrobat. Do not use a black marker — a marker can be scanned through and the underlying text recovered. Verify that redacted content is permanently removed before sending. If you are unsure how to do this, ask your medical provider's records department for assistance.

The at-fault insurer may claim they cannot process your claim without your complete unredacted records. In most states this is not true. If they threaten to deny your claim based on incomplete records, contact a personal injury attorney before you give them anything more.

Under HIPAA and most state laws, you have the right to protect unrelated medical information from disclosure. The at-fault insurance company does not get a free fishing trip through your entire medical history. They get records related to your crash injuries and nothing more.

■ Lost Wages and Income Documentation

If your injuries caused you to miss work, you are entitled to be compensated for that lost income. Documenting it properly is essential.

Gather the following:

- Recent pay stubs and W-2s from the prior two years to establish your pre-crash income
- A written letter from your employer confirming your missed work dates, your hourly rate or salary, and your typical hours
- Records of any sick leave, PTO, or vacation days you used to cover missed work — you should be reimbursed for these because those benefits were effectively consumed by the crash
- If you are an independent contractor, provide 1099s and income statements showing your typical earnings

> **Do not provide your tax returns to the insurance company without first consulting a personal injury attorney. For employees, your W-2s and employer verification letter are sufficient. For business owners, tax returns may be the only way to prove income loss, but releasing them without legal guidance can seriously complicate your case.**

Create a simple spreadsheet showing the dates you missed work, the hours missed each day, and your hourly wage. Multiply the hours by your rate to calculate your total lost wage claim. This gives the insurance company a clear, verifiable number to work with.

■ Long-Term and Permanent Income Loss

If your injuries have resulted in long-term physical limitations that affect your ability to work — you can no longer perform certain job duties, you had to accept a lower-paying position, or you missed a promotion due to medical appointments or surgery recovery — these losses are compensable and need to be documented.

Medical documentation from your treating physician stating your physical limitations is the foundation of this claim. In more severe cases, vocational experts and economists can calculate the long-term impact of your injuries on your earning capacity. These experts assess your age, occupation, experience, and injury severity to project future income loss.

> **Vocational expert reports typically cost $1,000 to $3,500 or more. If your injuries are severe enough to require this type of expert, you should be hiring a personal injury attorney. Cases involving permanent income loss are too complex and too valuable to handle without professional legal representation.**

■ Photographic and Video Evidence

> **YOUR SAFETY IS THE PRIMARY CONCERN AT A CRASH SCENE. Do not risk further injury attempting to obtain photographs or video. Only document the scene if it is safe to do so.**

Visual evidence is among the most powerful documentation in a car crash case. A picture is worth a thousand words — and a video is worth even more. Insurance companies find it very difficult to dispute what is clearly visible in a photograph or recording.

■ Photos to Take at the Scene

If you are able to do so safely, photograph the scene thoroughly from multiple angles:

- All vehicles involved — overall shots from every angle, then close-ups of specific damage
- License plates of every vehicle involved
- The at-fault driver's license, insurance card, and registration — photograph the documents directly

- Road conditions, skid marks, debris fields, fluids on the roadway
- Traffic signs, signals, and intersections
- Weather and visibility conditions
- The interior of your vehicle — deployed airbags, damage to the steering wheel, dashboard, or seats
- Your visible injuries — bruises, cuts, swelling, road rash — as soon as possible after the crash

> **Photograph the inside of your car. Interior photos frequently reveal the true severity of the impact in ways that exterior shots do not. Deployed airbags, cracked dashboards, bent steering columns, and deformed door panels tell the story of the forces your body absorbed.**

■ Ongoing Injury Documentation

Do not stop photographing after the crash scene. Continue photographing your injuries over time — bruising often darkens and spreads significantly in the days after a crash, and swelling may worsen before it improves. These progression photos document the ongoing physical impact of your injuries.

Once your healing is complete, photograph any permanent changes to your body — scarring, skin discoloration, surgical scars, or visible deformity. You are entitled to compensation for permanent crash-caused changes to your body, and photographic documentation of those changes is powerful evidence.

■ Video Evidence

Record a video walkthrough of the crash scene if you can safely do so, narrating as you go. Identify where your vehicle was struck, point out skid marks, debris, and road conditions, and describe what you observe. Video provides continuity and context that a series of still photos cannot fully capture.

As your recovery progresses, consider recording periodic video updates showing how your injuries are affecting your daily life. Demonstrating limited range of motion, difficulty walking, or inability to perform routine tasks — narrated in your own voice, in your own home — gives the insurance company a realistic and human picture of your losses that is very difficult to dismiss.

> **Never edit, filter, crop, or enhance any photo or video you intend to use as evidence. Altered visual evidence is immediately suspicious to insurance companies and may be referred to their fraud investigation unit — called an SIU or Special Investigations Unit. If your case goes to an SIU, you will almost certainly need an attorney to get it resolved.**

■ Organizing and Storing Visual Evidence

Create a dedicated folder on your phone and computer for all crash-related photos and videos. Use separate subfolders for scene photos, vehicle damage, and injury documentation. Label each file with the date and a brief description — for example, "2025-04-15 Crash Scene Front View" or "2025-04-22 Day 7 Bruising Right Shoulder."

Most smartphones automatically timestamp and geotag photos. This metadata is independent verification of when and where each photo was taken. Make sure location services are enabled on your phone when documenting the scene.

> **Back up your photos and videos to a secure cloud service immediately. Phones get lost, stolen, broken, or replaced. Losing your visual evidence because it only existed on one device is an entirely avoidable disaster.**

Complete, organized documentation of your medical care, income losses, and visual evidence is what separates a well-supported claim from one that gets lowballed or denied. Every record, every photo, every bill, and every employer letter is a piece of evidence that makes your case stronger and the insurance company's job of dismissing your claim harder. Build the file carefully. Build it completely. It will pay off.

Chapter 6

Dealing with Vehicle Repairs, Total Loss, and Rental Cars

After you have been evaluated by a doctor, your next immediate concern is your vehicle. Getting it repaired or replaced quickly, securing a rental car to maintain your mobility, and making sure you are paid fairly for your loss requires understanding how the insurance system works on the vehicle side of your claim.

This chapter covers your two options for handling vehicle repairs, how total loss determinations are made, what you are entitled to in a rental car, and how to avoid getting shortchanged at every step.

■ First: Notify Both Insurers of Your Vehicle's Location

Before anything else, call both the at-fault insurance company and your own insurance company and give each of them the exact address of wherever your vehicle currently sits — the tow yard, body shop, or storage facility.

> **Storage fees accumulate fast — $75 to $150 per day or more at many tow yards. The at-fault insurer is responsible for those fees, but only if they know where the vehicle is and have the opportunity to move it to a free or reduced-cost storage facility. Notifying both carriers immediately removes their ability to use lack of knowledge as an excuse to deny or reduce storage cost coverage.**

Make both calls the same day as the crash if possible. Get the name of the person you spoke with at each company and note the date and time. Document that both carriers were notified.

■ Your Two Options: Your Own Insurance vs. the At-Fault Insurer

When it comes to getting your vehicle repaired or declared a total loss, you have two paths: use your own collision insurance, or work directly with the at-fault driver's insurance. Each has real advantages and disadvantages. Here is an honest breakdown of both.

▪ Using Your Own Insurance

Your own insurance company has a contractual obligation to you. That contract is the single biggest advantage of going through your own insurer. They are required to act in good faith and process your claim promptly. The at-fault driver's insurance company has no contract with you and no legal obligation to prioritize your interests.

Practical advantages of using your own insurance:

- Faster processing and repair start — your insurer does not have to wait for a liability determination before authorizing repairs
- Higher total loss payout — your insurer's contractual duty to you typically produces a better settlement offer than the at-fault insurer
- Access to preferred repair shops with quality guarantees, though you generally have the right to choose your own shop
- Once repairs are complete, your insurer will pursue the at-fault insurer for reimbursement through subrogation and return your deductible to you when successful

> **Using your own insurance should not raise your rates if you were not at fault. In most states, including Colorado, insurers are prohibited from issuing an accident surcharge or chargeable incident when the insured was not responsible for the crash. Confirm this rule with a local attorney for your specific state.**

The primary disadvantage is that you must pay your deductible upfront. If the at-fault driver has adequate insurance, you will get it back — but you need to have it available immediately. Your insurer may also have the contractual right to use aftermarket parts rather than original equipment manufacturer (OEM) parts for repairs. Check your policy or ask your agent about this before approving any repair work.

■ Using the At-Fault Driver's Insurance

Going through the at-fault insurer means no upfront deductible and, generally, the right to require OEM factory replacement parts rather than aftermarket components. You also typically have free choice of repair shop.

The significant disadvantages: the at-fault insurer will not approve or begin repairs until they have accepted liability — which means waiting for the police report, their own investigation, and their decision. If fault is disputed, that wait can stretch into weeks. If liability is denied entirely, you are back to using your own insurance and pursuing legal action.

> **Our general recommendation: use your own insurance. It is almost always faster, your contractual relationship with your own insurer protects you better, and the deductible will be returned to you. The speed advantage alone is usually worth it.**

■ Understanding Total Loss

A vehicle is declared a total loss when the cost to repair it exceeds a threshold percentage of its pre-crash value. That threshold varies by insurer and by state but is typically between 70% and 80%. In most cases, airbag deployment alone will push a vehicle into total loss territory regardless of the repair cost estimate.

Example: Your car is worth $12,000 before the crash. Repairs are estimated at $9,000. That is 75% of the vehicle's value. The insurance company will likely declare it a total loss.

> **The total loss value of your vehicle is its Actual Cash Value (ACV) — what it was worth in the market the instant before the crash. It is not what you paid for it. It is not what you owe on it. It is not what it would cost to replace it with a new vehicle. The ACV is the**

> **number the insurance company is legally required to pay, and it is frequently less than people expect.**

■ How the ACV Is Calculated

Insurers calculate ACV based on your vehicle's make, model, year, condition, mileage, and comparable vehicles currently for sale in your market. They use proprietary internal data systems with thousands of data points. This is not a negotiation where being persuasive will move the number significantly.

What can legitimately increase the ACV offer:

- Recent upgrades or repairs — new tires, new brakes, a new stereo, a recent engine rebuild. Provide receipts. Insurers will generally consider items installed within one year before the crash.
- Comparable vehicle listings — search online for vehicles with the same year, make, model, condition, and mileage as yours and document the asking prices. If comparable vehicles in your market are consistently priced higher than the insurer's offer, that is evidence worth presenting.

> **It generally makes little sense to pay an independent appraiser $500 to $1,000 to dispute a total loss offer unless the difference between the offer and the true market value significantly exceeds that cost. Do the math before you hire an appraiser.**

■ Keeping a Totaled Vehicle

In some cases you may have the option to retain your totaled vehicle. The insurer pays you the ACV minus the vehicle's salvage value, and you keep the car. Be aware of what this means: you are personally responsible for all repairs, the vehicle must pass a state safety inspection before it can return to the road, and it will be re-titled with a salvage or branded title designation. A salvage title significantly reduces the vehicle's resale value and can affect your ability to insure it at standard rates going forward.

■ Diminished Value Claims

If your vehicle is repaired rather than totaled, it is worth less after the crash than it was before — even if the repairs are perfect. This reduction in value is called diminished value, and in many states you are entitled to compensation for it from the at-fault insurer.

To establish a diminished value claim, you need to show the difference between what your vehicle was worth before the crash and what a comparable repaired vehicle is worth in your market. One practical method: ask a local dealer who sells your brand of vehicle to provide a written statement of how much value a crash history reduces on that make and model. You can also search online listings for the same year, make, model, and condition — find one with no crash history and one with a crash-and-repaired history and document the price difference.

> **Diminished value claims generally do not apply to total loss vehicles — only to repaired vehicles. Submit your diminished value documentation to the at-fault insurer in writing along with a specific dollar demand. Be precise. Vague requests get vague responses.**

■ Your Right to a Rental Car

You are entitled to a rental car while your vehicle is being repaired or while you wait for a total loss settlement. Both your own insurance (if you purchased rental coverage) and the at-fault insurer's liability coverage may apply.

> **Rental car coverage is not part of "full coverage." If you did not buy it, you do not have it through your own insurance. However, in most states the at-fault driver's liability insurance is responsible for your**

rental costs regardless of whether you carry rental coverage yourself.

■ Rental Through Your Own Insurance

If you purchased rental reimbursement coverage, your insurer will cover rental costs up to your policy's daily and maximum limits for the duration of repairs or until a total loss settlement is reached, typically subject to a 30-day cap. Review your policy or call your agent to confirm your specific limits.

■ Rental Through the At-Fault Insurer

In most states, the at-fault driver's liability insurance is responsible for providing you with a rental vehicle comparable to the one that was damaged — not a downgrade. If your vehicle was a full-size truck or SUV, they cannot require you to drive a compact car.

The at-fault insurer is generally responsible for your rental costs for the full repair period — until your car is back in your hands from the body shop. If your car is a total loss, they owe you a rental until you receive your settlement check. Some insurers will attempt to cut off rental coverage before repairs are complete or before the settlement is paid. Push back. Document the start and end dates of your rental and keep every receipt.

At the time of publishing most insurance companies arrange rentals through Enterprise. The insurer will set up the reservation and provide you with a contract number. You take that number to the rental location and they get you a vehicle. You should not be paying out of pocket for a rental arranged this way.

One important note: if you are under 25 years old, the at-fault insurer is still responsible for any age-related surcharges the rental company charges. That additional cost is their obligation, not yours. However, insurance companies are generally not required to arrange a rental for drivers under 18.

Get written confirmation from the insurer — or at minimum an email — before agreeing to any rental terms. Confirm the daily rate, the duration covered, and whether the insurer is handling payment directly with the rental company. Verbal commitments from insurance adjusters are not reliable. Get it in writing.

Your vehicle is one of the most tangible and immediate losses after a crash. Understanding your rights around repairs, total loss valuations, and rental cars ensures you are not shortchanged on any of them. Move quickly, document everything, and push back when the insurance company tries to limit what they owe you.

Chapter 7

Communicating and Negotiating with Insurance Adjusters

Insurance adjusters are not your friends. They are not your enemies either. They are professionals doing a job — and that job is to close your claim for as little money as possible. Understanding who you are dealing with, how they think, and what tactics they use is the foundation of every successful negotiation.

This chapter covers the different types of adjusters you will encounter, how to present your case effectively, what to avoid, and how to negotiate a counteroffer without undermining yourself.

■ Understanding the Types of Adjusters

You will likely deal with multiple adjusters across different parts of your claim. Each one has a different role and a different relationship with you.

■ The Liability (BI) Adjuster

The liability or bodily injury adjuster works for the at-fault driver's insurance company. They have no contractual obligation to you and no legal duty to protect your interests. Their job is to evaluate your claim, find reasons to minimize it, and close it for as little as possible.

Many people are surprised by how friendly and sympathetic liability adjusters are in the early stages of a claim. Do not mistake that friendliness for advocacy. It is a strategy. The warmth frequently disappears the moment you stop accepting small offers or start asking hard questions about policy limits.

> **The liability adjuster's standard opening offer is often the total cost of your medical bills plus $2,500 or less for pain and suffering. This is a lowball offer designed to see if you will take the first number they give you. Do not accept it. It almost never reflects the full value of your case.**

■ The UM/UIM and MedPay Adjuster

Your own insurance company's UM/UIM and MedPay adjusters operate under a different legal standard. In many states, including Colorado, your own insurer is required by law to place your interests on equal footing with the company's interests when handling your first-party claims. Failure to do so — through lowball offers, unreasonable delays, or improper claim denials — can constitute insurance bad faith, which exposes your insurer to liability beyond the policy limits.

> **If your own insurance company is handling your UM/UIM or MedPay claim in bad faith — offering unreasonably low amounts, delaying without justification, or refusing to pay what is clearly owed — call a personal injury attorney immediately. Bad faith claims against insurers are complex but can result in significant additional compensation beyond your policy limits.**

■ The Property Damage (PD) Adjuster

The PD adjuster handles your vehicle repair or total loss claim. Their valuations are heavily data-driven — they run your VIN through proprietary systems that factor in mileage, condition, recent sales of comparable vehicles, and local market data. There is generally limited room for persuasive negotiation on vehicle values. As discussed in Chapter 7, your best path for vehicle claims is through your own insurance whenever possible.

■ How to Present Your Case

How you communicate with adjusters matters as much as what you say. Here are the principles that consistently produce better outcomes.

■ Stay Organized and Professional

Before you pick up the phone to discuss your claim, have everything in front of you — your medical records and bills organized chronologically, your lost wage documentation, your photos, your communication log. An adjuster who senses you are unprepared will use that to their advantage. An adjuster who can see you have a complete, organized file will treat your claim more seriously.

> **Never threaten to hire a lawyer. If you need one, hire one. Threats change nothing — insurance companies are sued thousands of times every day. It is a cost of doing business to them. Empty threats signal that you are frustrated and easily rattled, which tells an experienced adjuster you may not make a credible witness at trial. That weakens your position, not theirs.**

■ Stick to Facts and Documented Evidence

When discussing your injuries and losses with an adjuster, stay anchored to what your medical records and bills actually say. Do not use emotional language. Do not exaggerate. Do not speculate about injuries you have not yet been diagnosed with.

Instead of saying "I'm in pain all the time," say: "My treating physician documented ongoing pain at every visit from the date of the crash through my last appointment. The MRI confirmed a herniated disk at L4-L5. My doctor has stated the injury is permanent."

The difference between those two statements in the eyes of an adjuster is enormous. One is a complaint. The other is a documented, verifiable fact.

■ Know the Value of Your Claim Before You Call

Do not enter a negotiation without knowing your numbers. Add up your total medical bills, your lost wages, your mileage to and from medical appointments, and any out-of-pocket costs related to the crash.

Calculate your non-economic damages using the method described in Chapter 9. Know your total before the adjuster makes their first offer.

> **If you do not know what your claim is worth before you pick up the phone, you cannot negotiate effectively. The adjuster knows exactly what your bills add up to. You should too.**

■ What to Avoid: Recorded Statements and Broad Releases

■ Recorded Statements

The liability adjuster will almost certainly ask you for a recorded statement early in the claims process. Politely decline.

Here is exactly how this goes wrong: the day after the crash, you give a recorded statement and say you are "just a little sore." Three days later your pain has significantly worsened and an MRI reveals a herniated disk. When you attempt to settle months later, the adjuster pulls out your recorded statement and reminds you that you described your injuries as minor. Those words become their primary argument that you were not seriously hurt.

> **Politely declining a recorded statement to the liability adjuster will not hurt your case. They may tell you it will — that is not true. They can determine fault from the police report and from their own insured. You are not required to give them a recorded statement. Simply say: "I'm not comfortable giving a recorded statement at this time."**

The rule is simple: Liability adjuster = politely decline. Your own UM/UIM or MedPay adjuster = cooperate and give the statement. Your contract with your own insurer requires your cooperation. Failure to cooperate with your own insurer can give them grounds to deny your claim.

■ Medical and Employment Record Releases

The same rule applies to authorization forms for medical and employment records. Do not sign releases for the liability adjuster. Do sign them for your own UM/UIM or MedPay adjuster.

> **Be especially cautious of releases the liability adjuster describes as "limited" to crash-related records. Healthcare providers are not going to review your records line by line to filter out unrelated items before sending them. Once you sign a release, you have no control over what gets sent.**
>
> **Unrelated medical history in the hands of the liability adjuster is never in your interest and can be used to devalue your claim.**

■ Avoiding Premature Settlement

Adjusters are trained to offer early settlements before the full picture of your injuries and losses is clear. An offer made within 90 days of the crash or within 60 days of your last medical treatment is almost always premature.

> **Never settle before you know the full extent of your injuries. We have had many clients who believed they were fully healed, settled their case, and within 60 days had their pain return — some temporarily, some permanently. Once you sign a release and accept a settlement, your case is closed forever. There is no coming back.**

Wait until you have reached maximum medical improvement — the point at which your doctors have determined that your condition is as good as it is going to get, whether that means full recovery or a permanent injury. Only then do you have a complete picture of what your case is actually worth.

■ Making a Counteroffer

The initial offer from the liability adjuster is a starting point, not a final number. It is designed to be low enough that some people accept it immediately. Your job is to respond with a documented, professional counteroffer.

■ Know Your Range Before You Respond

Before you respond to any offer, establish two numbers in your mind: your minimum acceptable settlement — the absolute floor below which you will not go without hiring an attorney — and your target settlement, which represents the full value of your documented losses plus fair non-economic damages. Your counteroffer should be at or above your target, not at your floor.

■ Put Your Counteroffer in Writing

Do not negotiate orally if you can avoid it. A written counter-offer letter forces you to think through your position clearly, without the pressure of a live conversation, and creates a documented record of your position.

Your letter should include:

- A specific dollar amount for your total medical bills
- Mileage and out-of-pocket expenses
- Lost wages with supporting documentation
- A specific calculation and dollar amount for your non-economic damages
- A total settlement demand
- A deadline — typically 30 days — for the insurer to respond

Keep the letter factual, professional, and free of emotional language. Do not exaggerate. Do not threaten. Let the numbers do the work.

■ Ask for a Written Explanation of Their Offer

If the adjuster's offer remains significantly below your documented losses, ask them to provide a written explanation of how they valued your claim. This documentation reveals whether they are overlooking expenses, applying improper discounts, or ignoring portions of your claim entirely. It also gives you something concrete to take to a personal injury attorney if you decide you need one.

■ Handling Pressure Tactics

Adjusters are trained negotiators. They will use tactics designed to create urgency, exploit uncertainty, and pressure you into settling quickly. Here is what to watch for.

> **The only real deadline in your case is the Statute of Limitations — the legal cutoff after which you can no longer file a lawsuit against the at-fault party. Statutes of limitations vary by state and can be as short as one year. An adjuster's "limited time offer" is almost always fabricated. The SOL is not. Know the SOL in your state and make sure your case is resolved — or in the hands of an attorney — well before it expires.**

If you plan to hire an attorney, do so at least nine months before the SOL expires, and a year is better. Attorneys need time to review your case, obtain records, and prepare for litigation. Do not wait until the last month.

When an adjuster senses frustration or impatience, they will slow down. When they sense confidence and preparation, they tend to move. Stay calm, stay organized, and be willing to walk away from an insufficient offer. You do not need to announce that you are walking away or that you are hiring an attorney — simply stop accepting inadequate offers and let your actions speak.

■ Document Every Communication

Keep a written log of every interaction with every adjuster. For each contact, record the date, time, the adjuster's name and direct phone number, and a summary of what was discussed and what was agreed to. Use email whenever possible to create an automatic written record.

> **"<u>If it is not in writing, it never happened.</u>" This legal principle applies to every stage of your claim. Verbal commitments from adjusters are not enforceable. Every agreement — a settlement amount, a repair authorization, and a rental car extension — must be confirmed in writing before you rely on it.**

When you reach a settlement agreement, the written document must include: the total settlement amount, who is responsible for paying your medical bills and any subrogation obligations, a deadline for payment, and the specific claims being released. Review every line before you sign. Once you sign a settlement release, your case is permanently closed. What is not in the document will not be enforceable later.

Chapter 8

Valuing Your Case Beyond Medical Bills

Medical bills are the most visible part of your claim, but they are not the most important part. The full value of a car crash case includes everything the crash took from you — your comfort, your sleep, your relationships, your hobbies, your career trajectory, your sense of self. These are called non-economic damages, and in many cases they represent the majority of what your case is actually worth.

This chapter explains how to identify, document, and present your non-economic damages — including what we call the human damages framework, which is the foundation of how the best personal injury trial attorneys in the country value cases.

■ What Are Non-Economic Damages?

Non-economic damages are the losses that do not come with a receipt. Insurance companies sometimes call them, "General Damages"; they are the same thing. They include:

- Physical pain and suffering — the ongoing discomfort, aching, and limitations caused by your injuries
- Mental and emotional distress — anxiety, depression, PTSD, sleep disruption, and fear
- Loss of enjoyment of life — the activities, hobbies, and experiences you can no longer participate in or can only do in a diminished way
- Inconvenience — the daily friction that your injuries add to ordinary tasks
- Loss of consortium — in most states, only a legally married spouse can bring a loss of consortium claim. The claim generally does not extend to domestic or civil partnerships, or to children. The laws vary widely by state. Check your local laws or consult a personal injury attorney in your state for advice on whether this claim applies to your situation.
- Permanent impairment or disfigurement — scarring, permanent physical limitation, or any lasting change to your body

Expect the insurance company and adjuster to minimize or entirely ignore your non-economic ("general") damages. It is their standard practice. Your job is to document these damages so thoroughly and specifically that they cannot be dismissed.

■ The Problem with Multiplier Methods

For decades, many attorneys and insurance companies used a simple multiplier to estimate non-economic damages — take the total medical bills and multiply by 2.5 or 3. If your bills were $10,000, the formula produced a total claim value of $25,000 to $30,000 — meaning $10,000 for your medical bills and only $15,000 to $20,000 for your non-economic and impairment damages combined.

Multiplier Method Example (3x)

Medical Bills	$10,000
Non-Economic Damages	$7,500 – $10,000
Impairment/Disfigurement Damages	$7,500 – $10,000
Total Claim Value	**$25,000 – 30,000**

This method is arbitrary and almost always underestimates real human losses. Here is why.

If I told you in advance that I was going to rear-end your car and herniate a disk in your low back — that you would be in significant pain for at least a year regardless of how much treatment you received, that you would never get back to 100%, that you would not be able to sit or stand for more than ten minutes without increasing your pain, and that you would not sleep more than three hours at a stretch for the next twelve months — how much money would I have to pay you to volunteer for that injury?

> **$20,000 for a year of that suffering is not fair compensation. It is an insult. That is the fundamental problem with multiplier methods. They produce a number, not justice.**

Here is a real example from our practice. Medical bills: $40,000. Using a 3x multiplier, the total case value would have been $120,000 with $80,000 attributed to non-economic damages. The insurance company refused to offer even that. We took the case to trial.

The jury awarded over $500,000 in non-economic damages alone — more than twelve times what the multiplier method suggested was fair. The total recovery for our client was nearly $3,000,000.

> **If you are going to hire a personal injury attorney, ask them directly how they calculate non-economic damages. If they give you a multiplier, find a different attorney. If your current attorney is using a multiplier, get a second opinion. The multiplier method is a shortcut that benefits the insurance company, not you.**

■ The Per Diem Method: A Better Starting Point

A more accurate approach to estimating non-economic damages for the purposes of handling your own case is the per diem — or daily rate — method. Assign a dollar value to each day of your pain and suffering and multiply by the number of days you experienced it.

A reasonable starting point for the daily rate is your hourly wage on the day of the crash, multiplied by 16 hours — the number of waking hours in a day. Example: if you earn $20 per hour, your daily rate is $320. If you suffered significant pain and limitation for 180 days, your non-economic damage estimate is $57,600.

This method is not perfect either, but it grounds the calculation in something concrete and human — the actual cost of your time, translated into a measure of what your suffering is worth. It is far more defensible in a negotiation than a number produced by multiplying a bill.

The per diem method is a tool for your own settlement negotiation, not a ceiling on what your case is worth. A skilled trial attorney working with your full case facts may arrive at a significantly higher number. Use this method to establish a reasonable floor for your non-economic damage demand — not the final answer.

■ The Human Damages Framework: Documenting What the Crash Took From You

Human damages is the term we use internally at Fair Squared Injury Law to describe the full human cost of a crash — the impact on your daily life, your relationships, your career, your mental health, and your sense of who you are. Under the law these fall within non-economic damages. In practice, they are what move a jury.

The best way to capture human damages is through a detailed, consistent journal. What follows are the categories you should be documenting. Use these as prompts each time you write.

■ Daily Life and Physical Limitations

Be specific. Do not say "it is harder to do things around the house." Say: "I used to vacuum the entire house in 30 minutes. Today I had to stop three times because of pain in my neck and back. It took over an hour and I had to lie down afterward."

Document every physical limitation in concrete, specific terms. What could you do before the crash that you cannot do now? What can you still do, but only with pain, reduced capacity, or increased time? How has your sleep been affected? What does a bad pain day look like, hour by hour?

Equally important is documenting your good days and low-pain days. Insurance companies will seize on any evidence that you performed a physical activity as proof that you are not seriously injured. Your journal needs to tell the full story — including what happens after a good day. Did you attempt an activity you used to do easily, only to find you could only complete part of it? And did you pay for it over the days that followed?

Example: "I felt better today so we decided to go on a short hike. Before the crash we would normally plan for 5 miles and make a full day of it. Today I could only manage 2 miles before the pain in my back became too much. I thought I had taken it easy. For the next 2 to 3 days I was significantly sorer than usual — worse than on days I did nothing at all."

This is one of the most important things to capture in your journal. Yes, I can still do some of the things I did before the crash — but I pay for it for days afterward, even when I take it easy. That pattern of activity followed by prolonged increased pain is powerful evidence of the ongoing impact of your injuries. Document it every time it happens. And critically — tell your doctor about it at your next appointment. A journal entry is self-reported. A physician's note documenting that you reported increased pain following light activity is clinical evidence. When your journal and your medical records tell the same story, it becomes significantly harder for the insurance company to dismiss or deny.

> **Specific, detailed, personal writing is persuasive. Vague generalizations are not. The more precisely you describe the real impact of your injuries on real days of your real life, the harder it becomes for an insurance company to dismiss your non-economic damages as exaggerated or unproven.**

■ Relationships

Describe how the crash has changed your relationships with the people you love. Have you been less present with your children because of pain or fatigue? Has your relationship with your spouse or partner been strained by your physical limitations, your emotional state, or your inability to participate in activities you used to share? Have your friends noticed a change in you?

One area that is almost universally overlooked — and that you must document — is changes or limitations in sexual activity with your partner. This is uncomfortable for most people to discuss and write about. Do it anyway. Physical intimacy is a fundamental part of a healthy relationship, and crash-caused injuries frequently affect it directly — through pain, limited mobility, fatigue, or the emotional and psychological effects of trauma. When a crash takes that away from you, even partially, it is a real and significant loss.

In my experience trying cases, juries understand this deeply. They are real people with real relationships. When they hear that a crash victim can no longer connect physically with their spouse or partner because of pain or injury, they do not dismiss it. They feel it. It is one of the most human losses a crash can cause, and it consistently influences jury verdicts in ways that medical bill calculations never do.

Document it in your journal honestly and specifically. Tell your doctor. The embarrassment of writing it down is nothing compared to the cost of leaving it out.

These relationship impacts are real damages. They belong in your journal and in your settlement demand. Do not be embarrassed to write them down.

■ Career and Economic Impact Beyond Lost Wages

Lost wages are the direct financial loss from missed work. But the career impact of a serious crash often goes much deeper. Did you miss a promotion because you were attending medical appointments or recovering from surgery? Did you use all of your sick leave and vacation time — benefits that will take years to rebuild? Did your job performance suffer in documented ways because of ongoing pain or cognitive effects from a concussion? Did you lose clients or accounts because you could not meet their needs during your recovery?

These losses are compensable. Document them specifically and keep any written communications — emails from supervisors, performance reviews, client correspondence — that reflect the career impact of your injuries.

■ Mental Health

Car crashes are traumatic events. PTSD, anxiety, depression, and phobias related to driving or riding in vehicles are surprisingly common after serious crashes. They are even more likely if you sustained a concussion. These are legitimate medical conditions, not weakness, and they are compensable damages.

I want to share something personal here, because I think it matters.

I spent 22 years in law enforcement. I responded to hundreds of crashes. I have seen things that most people will never see. By any measure, I am not someone who rattles easily. And yet after the DUI driver rear-ended me, I suffered significant mental distress for over a year. Every time I stopped at a red light, I found myself nervously checking my mirrors — scanning for a car coming up behind me too fast, bracing for an impact that might be coming. Driving anxiety was something I had never experienced before in my life. It did not matter that I knew intellectually what had happened and why. My nervous system did not care about my credentials.

The point is this: it does not matter who you are or how tough you consider yourself. Mental distress after a crash is real, it is common, and it deserves to be taken seriously and documented. It does not make you weak. It makes you human. Document it in your journal and tell your doctors about it. Your mental health damages are a legitimate and compensable part of your case.

> **If your mental health has changed since the crash — you are anxious driving, you are not sleeping, you are experiencing mood changes, you are having intrusive thoughts about the crash — see a mental health professional and document it in your journal. Treatment not only helps you heal, it also substantiates your mental health damages to the insurance company.**

If you ever experience thoughts of self-harm or harming others, go to the emergency room or call 988, the Suicide and Crisis Lifeline, immediately. Help is available. **You are not alone.** These thoughts are a medical symptom, not a character flaw, and they deserve immediate professional attention.

▪ Permanent Changes to Your Body

If the crash left you with permanent injuries — a disk that will never fully heal, a surgical scar, metal hardware implanted in your spine or joints, a reduced range of motion that will be with you for the rest of your life — these are among the most significant damages in your entire claim. Permanent injuries are not just about what you suffer today. They are about every day for the rest of your life.

> **In most states you are entitled to compensation for permanent crash-caused changes to your body — physical impairment, disfigurement, and any future pain and suffering that will result from your permanent condition. These damages must be specifically identified and documented. Make sure your doctors are recording the permanency of your injuries clearly in your medical records.**

▪ Your Journal: The Most Powerful Non-Economic Evidence You Can Create

A pain and suffering journal is one of the most effective tools available to someone handling their own case. It creates a contemporaneous, dated record of your experience that is extremely difficult for an insurance company to dismiss.

Write in your journal regularly — ideally daily during your worst periods, and at minimum after any significant event that illustrates the impact of your injuries. Each entry should be dated and specific. Here is an example of an effective journal entry:

> *April 15 — Went hiking for the first time since the crash. I chose the easiest trail at the park, which I used to consider a warmup. I made it half a mile before my back pain became too severe to continue. I sat against a tree for about ten minutes, then slowly walked back to my car. By the time I got there, the pain was worse than when I stopped. I sat in the parking lot for 20 minutes before I felt safe to drive home. I used to hike 8 to 10 miles on difficult trails without thinking twice. Today half a mile broke me. I cried in the car.*

That entry is specific, personal, dated, and emotionally honest without being exaggerated. It tells a story. Stories move people — including insurance adjusters, mediators, and juries.

> **Your journal will become part of your case and will likely be reviewed by the insurance company. Write only about crash-related impacts. Do not include unrelated personal matters, complaints about people in your life unrelated to the crash, or anything you would be embarrassed to have read aloud in a courtroom. Everything in the journal should be true, specific, and directly connected to your crash-caused injuries and their effects.**

■ Statements from People Who Know You

Statements from family members, close friends, coworkers, or anyone who interacts with you regularly and has witnessed the changes the crash brought to your life can add significant weight to your non-economic damage claim. These are people with no financial stake in your case who can speak to who you were before and who you are now.

Ask them to write a brief, honest, specific statement describing what they have observed. What was he like before the crash? What is he like now? What specific things have they seen or heard that illustrate the change? Written statements from people who know you well are compelling evidence that is difficult for an insurance company to simply ignore.

Your medical bills tell the insurance company what the crash cost in dollars. Your journal, your statements, your documented limitations, and your human story tell them what the crash cost in life. Both matter. But in the cases where real justice gets done — in the cases where juries return verdicts that actually reflect what a person lost — it is always the human story that makes the difference.

Document yours carefully. It is worth more than you know.

Chapter 9

Finalizing Your Claim and Settling

You have completed your medical treatment, reached maximum medical improvement, gathered your documentation, and calculated your damages. Now it is time to give the insurance company a formal opportunity to resolve your claim. This is called a settlement demand, or more precisely, a settlement opportunity letter.

This chapter walks you through crafting that letter, understanding the negotiation process, and managing your settlement payout correctly from acceptance through final distribution.

■ Before You Write: Know Your Numbers

Before you put a single word on paper, you need to have three numbers clearly established.

The first is your total claim value — the full amount of your economic damages (medical bills, lost wages, mileage, out-of-pocket expenses) plus your non-economic damages (pain and suffering, inconvenience, loss of enjoyment of life, permanent impairment or disfigurement) calculated using the per diem method described in Chapter 9.

The second is your total subrogation obligations — every dollar you are legally required to pay back to health insurance, MedPay, Medicare, Medicaid, or any other insurer that paid on your behalf. These reduce what you actually keep from the settlement.

The third is your walk-away amount — the minimum dollar amount you will actually take home after all medical bills, co-pays, deductibles, and subrogation obligations are paid. This is your true floor. Do not accept a settlement that leaves you below it.

> **Know your walk-away amount before you send anything to the insurance company. If you do not know what you need to walk away with, you cannot negotiate effectively. Work backward: start with your walk-away target, add all payback obligations, and that gives you your minimum acceptable gross settlement. Everything above that is negotiating room.**

■ Crafting Your Settlement Opportunity Letter

The settlement opportunity letter is the document that formally presents your claim to the at-fault insurance company and gives them the opportunity to resolve it. A sample letter is included at the back of this book. Here is what every effective settlement letter must contain.

■ Opening: Who You Are and What You Want

Open with a clear, direct statement that you are seeking settlement for the damages you suffered as a result of the crash. Include the crash date, location, and your claim number. Keep it to two or three sentences. There is no need for a lengthy introduction.

■ Summary of the Crash and Liability

Provide a brief factual description of what happened and who was at fault. This section should be no more than two to three sentences. The police report will accompany your letter and speak for itself — there is no need to recap it in detail.

Example: "Your insured failed to stop in response to stopped traffic and struck the rear of my vehicle. The responding officer issued your insured a citation for careless driving. A copy of the police report is enclosed."

> **Do not write a novel about the crash. Two to three sentences establishing fault is sufficient. The police report, the citation, and your medical records do the heavy lifting. Your job in this section is simply to put the liability issue on the table clearly and move on.**

■ Description of Injuries and Treatment

Some attorneys will tell you to list every injury and every treatment in detail in the letter. We do not. You are sending the insurance company your complete medical bills and records. They are going to read them regardless of whether you summarize them in the letter. Save yourself the time and let the records speak for themselves.

What you should include is a brief statement that you sustained injuries requiring medical treatment, that you have enclosed all relevant medical bills and records, and that you have now reached maximum medical improvement.

■ Non-Economic Damages

This is the most important section of the letter. Describe in specific, personal terms how the crash has affected your life — your daily activities, your work, your relationships, your sleep, your mental health, and any permanent changes to your body. Draw directly from your journal. Use specific examples, not generalizations.

> **This is where your journal earns its value. Specific, personal, documented descriptions of how the crash changed your life are far more persuasive than generic statements about pain and suffering. The adjuster reading your letter has seen thousands of claims. Make yours human and specific enough that it is impossible to dismiss.**

■ Your Settlement Demand: Always Ask for the Full Global Policy Limits

Your settlement demand should always be for the full global available policy limits — regardless of the actual amount, regardless of whether you know what the limits are, and regardless of whether your damages equal the limits.

There are several reasons for this. You frequently will not know the exact policy limits. Asking for the global limits ensures you do not accidentally leave money on the table by naming a specific number that is lower than the available coverage. It gives you maximum negotiating room. And if you eventually need to hire an attorney, this critical step is already completed, which can accelerate your case.

Always ask for the full global available policy limits. Always. Even if your medical bills are $5,000 and the policy is $100,000, ask for the full limits. You are not obligated to accept less, and you are not harmed by asking for more. The insurance company will tell you what they are willing to pay. Your job is to ask for everything available.

▪ Response Deadline

Close the letter by requesting a response within 35 days from the date you send it. Do not give less than 30 days — courts have found that unreasonably short response windows can invalidate a settlement demand. Include your mailing address and email address clearly so there is no ambiguity about where the response should be sent.

Do not accept any settlement offers made verbally over the phone. There is no written proof of a verbal offer and verbal commitments are not enforceable. Instruct the adjuster that all offers must be made in writing. If they make a verbal offer, respond in writing: "Thank you for your offer of $xx,xxx. Please confirm in writing so I may consider it."

▪ Sending Your Letter and Documents

Send your settlement letter, medical bills and records, police report, lost wage documentation, and any other supporting materials by email or fax. Email is preferred because it creates an automatic timestamped record. Some insurance companies will email you a link to upload your documents and settlement letter directly to their system; others accept them via email or fax. Do not send your materials by mail, and politely reject any request from the insurance company to submit your settlement offer that way. This is the 21st century — nobody uses the mail to send settlement offers, and doing so only slows your case down and reduces your ability to confirm timely receipt. Put your claim number on every document you send. Follow up with a brief email confirming receipt if you do not receive an acknowledgment within a few days.

Put your claim number on every single communication with every insurance company — every email, every fax, every letter, every document. Insurance companies handle thousands of claims at once. Without your claim number, documents get lost, delayed, or filed under the wrong account. A missing claim number is one of the most common and most avoidable reasons a settlement gets delayed. Make it the first thing on every page you send.

Send the same package to your own insurance company at the same time. Let them know you have submitted a settlement demand to the at-fault insurer and ask them to evaluate any amounts owed to you under your own UM/UIM or MedPay coverage. Critically, most UM/UIM policies require you to obtain your own insurer's written permission before you settle with the at-fault carrier. Include a specific written request for that permission in your letter. Settling with the at-fault insurer without first obtaining your UM/UIM carrier's consent can void your UM/UIM coverage entirely, potentially costing you thousands of dollars in coverage you paid for and are entitled to. Do not skip this step.

Most UM/UIM policies require your own insurer's written consent before you settle with the at-fault carrier. When you send your settlement package to your own insurance company, include an explicit written request for permission to settle. Do not accept any settlement funds from the at-fault insurer until you have that written consent in hand. Settling without it can void your UM/UIM coverage permanently. Read your policy or call your insurer to confirm their specific consent requirements before you settle anything.

■ Receiving and Negotiating the Settlement Offer

The at-fault insurance company will typically respond before your deadline expires, usually by email. Unless they are offering the full policy limits, the first offer will almost always be low — typically your medical bills plus a token amount of $2,000 or less for pain and suffering. Do not be insulted and do not be rattled. This is standard practice. It is a starting point, not a final answer.

> **If the insurance company offers you the full global policy limits in response to your demand letter, you should generally accept. In most cases the at-fault driver does not have significant personal assets beyond their insurance coverage. A policy limits offer is frequently the best available outcome, and rejecting it to pursue a lawsuit against an underinsured defendant is rarely worth the time, cost, and risk.**

■ The Three-Offer Negotiation Method

Negotiation over the phone with a trained insurance adjuster is not recommended unless you have significant negotiating experience. Adjusters negotiate claims for a living. Written negotiation via email gives you time to think, keeps a clear record, and removes the pressure of a live conversation.

One straightforward method for structuring your counteroffers is the three-offer approach. Start by establishing your true minimum — this becomes your third and final offer. Then add 50% to arrive at your second offer. Add 50% to that to arrive at your first offer.

Example: Your minimum acceptable settlement is $5,000. Your second offer is $7,500. Your first counteroffer is $11,500.

> **Never reveal your final number before you make your third offer. The moment the adjuster knows your floor, negotiation is over. You will get your floor**

> **and nothing more. Hold it back until the third offer and not a moment sooner.**

Here is how that negotiation might look in practice:

Adjuster: *We received your demand for the policy limits. We don't value your claim at the policy limits, but we're willing to offer $2,000 as full and final settlement.*

You: *I appreciate the response, but I can't settle for that amount. I'll settle for $11,500.*

Adjuster: *[Provides reasons your claim isn't worth $11,500.] We can go to $3,000.*

You: *I appreciate you coming up, but that won't get it done. I'll settle for $7,500 and release your insured from all claims.*

Adjuster: *[More pushback.] I don't have much more room, but I can go to $4,250.*

You: *Make it $5,000 and we have a deal.*

Adjuster: *Let me speak with my supervisor. [Returns.] We'll do $5,000.*

Every case and every adjuster are different. This example illustrates one possible path. The principles — start high, move in calculated steps, never reveal your floor early — apply in every negotiation.

For a deeper understanding of negotiation principles, I recommend the book Never Split the Difference by Chris Voss. I receive nothing for that recommendation. It has genuinely helped my team and I get better results, and it will help you too.

■ Accepting the Settlement and Reviewing the Agreement

Once you reach an agreed settlement amount, everything stops until you have the written settlement agreement in hand. Do not make any payments, do not call anyone, and do not consider the matter resolved until you have reviewed and signed a written agreement.

Read every line of the settlement agreement before you sign it. The agreement must include: the exact settlement amount, who is responsible for paying your medical providers and subrogation obligations, a payment deadline, and the specific claims being released. If an agreed-upon term is not in the written document, it does not exist. What you sign is what you get — nothing more.

If any part of the agreement is unclear or does not reflect what you agreed to, do not sign it. Ask the adjuster for a corrected version. If you are uncertain about the legal language, the cost of one hour with a personal injury attorney to review the agreement is money extremely well spent. A misunderstood release can close the door permanently on claims you did not intend to settle.

■ Managing Subrogation and Final Distribution

Before you distribute any settlement funds, you must resolve every subrogation obligation. Contact every insurer or program that paid on your behalf and obtain a final payback amount in writing. The document should use language like "final settlement," "final subrogation amount," or "final lien." These letters typically expire after 30 days, so move promptly once you have them.

WARNING: Failing to repay Medicare, Medicaid, or Medicare Advantage is not a technicality — it is a serious federal matter. These programs will find out about your settlement because all insurers are required by law to report it. Failure to repay them can result in denial of your future benefits, legal action to recover the full amount, and payment of their attorney's fees on top of what you owe. Pay them. Get proof of payment. Keep it forever.

Once all final subrogation amounts are confirmed in writing, distribute the settlement funds in this order: pay all medical providers with outstanding balances, pay all subrogation obligations, pay any remaining co-pays and deductibles, and keep the remainder. Pay by check or credit card so you have proof of every payment. Keep copies of everything.

■ A Note on Taxes

Tax treatment of personal injury settlements is beyond the scope of this book. Most personal injury awards are not taxable, but there are exceptions — particularly for punitive damages, interest on the settlement, and compensation for lost wages. Do not assume your settlement is tax-free without getting advice from a qualified tax professional.

Consult a tax professional about the taxability of your settlement before you spend the money. Failing to pay taxes owed on any taxable portion of your settlement will subject you to penalties, interest, and potentially much worse. The cost of a tax consultation is trivial compared to the cost of getting this wrong.

Finalizing your claim is the culmination of everything you have done since the day of the crash. Every medical appointment you attended, every record you collected, every journal entry you wrote, every phone call you documented — it all comes together here. Take your time, do it right, and make sure every dollar you are owed ends up where it belongs: with you.

Chapter 10

When to Consider Hiring a Lawyer

This book has been honest with you throughout about when you can handle your own case and when you cannot. Chapter 1 gave you the initial list of situations that require an attorney. This chapter goes deeper — explaining why those situations require legal representation, what to look for in a personal injury trial attorney, and how to avoid the most common and costly mistakes people make when choosing one.

■ When the Insurance Company Will Not Move

There comes a point in some cases where no amount of documentation, no number of phone calls, and no additional evidence will change the insurance company's position. When you reach that point, you have two choices: accept what they are offering, or hire an experienced trial attorney to file a lawsuit.

Insurance companies are not going to suddenly realize they were wrong and increase their offer because you argued persuasively. They are a multi-trillion-dollar industry. Your case is not personal to them. It is a claim to be closed for as little money as possible. The only thing that reliably changes their calculus is the credible threat of a trial verdict that costs them significantly more than a fair settlement would have.

> **The one thing insurance companies genuinely fear is losing their money to an experienced trial attorney with a proven history of taking cases to verdict and winning. Not a lawyer who threatens to sue. Not a lawyer who sends strongly worded letters. An attorney with an actual trial record that insurance companies know, respect, and fear. That is the only leverage that consistently moves them off their position.**

■ The Trial Experience Requirement

When this book says you need a personal injury attorney, it means a personal injury **trial attorney** — someone whose primary practice is injury law and who has actual, recent jury trial experience. This distinction matters enormously and most people do not know how to ask about it.

Approximately half of all personal injury attorneys have never taken a case to trial and jury verdict. I have seen this firsthand at trainings and conventions — ask the room how many attorneys have tried a case to verdict in the last two years, and roughly half the hands stay down. An attorney who has never tried a case — or who has not tried one in the last five years — is not a threat to the insurance company. They know it. Their adjusters know it. And they will treat your case accordingly.

The first question to ask any personal injury attorney you are considering hiring: "How many cases have you tried to verdict in the last two years?"

If the answer is zero, or if they hedge and change the subject, thank them for their time and call someone else. An attorney without recent trial experience cannot get full value on your case because the insurance company has no reason to fear them.

A note on verdicts: In the last three years I have taken six cases all the way to jury verdict. That history creates a significant and measurable risk for insurance companies. They know that if they do not settle for a full and fair amount, the case goes to trial — and my track record means they cannot predict the outcome in their favor. The way insurance companies eliminate that risk is by settling before trial begins. Insurance companies do not let cases go to verdict against attorneys who have a track record of obtaining large verdicts against them. When your lawyer has a proven record, cases settle — favorably — before a jury ever gets to decide. That is the goal.

My most recent example: the at-fault insurer's final offer — their "take it or try the case" number — was $225,000. My client wanted $400,000, which was honestly still conservative in my assessment of the case's value. Her motivation was not greed. It was

> **what she believed was fair. The case settled on a Friday afternoon at 3:00 p.m. — for the full $400,000. Trial was set to begin the following Monday at 8:30 a.m.**

Also, do not make the mistake of hiring a family member or friend who is a lawyer in a different area of practice. A real estate attorney, a family law attorney, or a business attorney may be an excellent lawyer in their field. They are not equipped to handle the rules, discovery requirements, expert witness management, trial strategy, or the significant costs of personal injury litigation that a serious personal injury lawsuit demands. Hiring the wrong attorney can be worse than handling the lawsuit yourself.

> **Hiring a non-personal injury attorney for your personal injury lawsuit is a critical error. In many cases you are genuinely better off handling the lawsuit yourself than handing it to an attorney who is out of their depth. If you are going to hire an attorney, hire the right one.**

▪ Specific Situations That Require a Trial Attorney

▪ Low or Insulting Settlement Offers

If the insurance company's offer does not cover your medical bills, lost wages, and a reasonable amount for your pain and suffering, you are being lowballed. An experienced trial lawyer is the most effective tool available for breaking that impasse. In most cases, the mere retention of a credible trial attorney changes the dynamic of the negotiation before a lawsuit is even filed.

> **Real example: I took on a case where the insurance company's final offer — their stated maximum — was $7,000. After I got involved and gave them one last opportunity to pay the policy limits before I filed a lawsuit, the offer went to $25,000. The full policy**

> **limits. Their "top" offer had been less than a third of what they were actually required to pay. That is not an anomaly. That is standard practice.**

■ Serious or Complex Injuries

Surgeries, spinal injuries, traumatic brain injuries, permanent disabilities, and any injury requiring long-term or future medical care are too complex and too valuable to handle without professional legal representation. These cases require medical experts, life care planners, and economists to properly calculate and present the full scope of your damages. An experienced trial attorney knows which experts to hire, how to use them effectively, and which ones to avoid.

> **Real example: A young woman turned left in front of my 55-year-old client. He spent a week in the hospital followed by five weeks in an inpatient physical rehabilitation facility. The case required multiple treating physicians, medical experts, and an accident reconstructionist, along with the credible threat of a multi-million-dollar verdict. It settled before a lawsuit was ever filed — for the full $1,250,000 policy limits.**
>
> **Without an experienced trial attorney, that case would have settled for a fraction of that amount.**

■ Disputed Liability

If the other driver or their insurer is disputing fault — claiming you were partially or fully responsible for the crash — you need an attorney. We have seen insurance companies insist a client was 25% at fault when the law in their state clearly established they were 0% at fault. It took retaining our firm to force them to accept full responsibility and pay the claim. You cannot effectively litigate comparative fault without legal representation.

Real example: A client came to me after the insurance company told him he was 20% at fault because he did not stop fast enough before their insured backed into him at high speed. One email from me changed everything. The at-fault insurer accepted 100% liability and paid the claim in full. The client had accepted their version of events as legitimate. It was not.

Some liability disputes cannot be resolved through negotiation regardless of how strong your case is. When that happens there are only two options: hire an attorney to file a lawsuit and take the case to trial, or accept the fault percentage (and the reduced settlement) being assigned to you by the insurance company. Only an experienced trial attorney can effectively pursue the first option.

▪ Insurance Company Bad Faith Tactics

Unreasonable delays, outright denials without legitimate basis, lowball offers that bear no relationship to your documented damages, bogus assignments of fault to you, and high-pressure tactics designed to force a quick settlement are all potential indicators of bad faith claims handling. An experienced trial attorney not only knows how to counter these tactics — they have seen every one of them before and are not intimidated by any of them.

Real example: A chiropractor referred a patient to me because the insurance company had told her there was only $25,000 in coverage and was refusing to respond to her calls about repairing her vehicle. When I got involved I discovered there was actually $75,000 in bodily injury coverage, plus an additional $25,000 in property damage coverage for her car. The at-fault insurer paid every penny of every available limit. She went from being told she would receive almost nothing to a $100,000 total payout. The insurance company had simply lied about the

available coverage and counted on her not knowing any better. Past results are not a guarantee of future outcomes and every case is different — but this case illustrates exactly why you need someone in your corner who knows what to look for.

■ Complex Legal or Insurance Rules

Comparative fault laws, statutes of limitations, Medicare and Medicaid set-aside requirements, UM/UIM claim procedures, and PIP or MedPay claim rules vary significantly from state to state and are frequently misrepresented by insurance companies. If your case involves any of these complexities, an attorney who practices personal injury law daily is the only reliable source of accurate guidance.

A word of caution on Google searches and AI programs: do not rely on either for legal advice about your specific case. Search engines surface general information that may be outdated, written for a different state, or simply wrong. AI programs — including the most sophisticated ones available today — can generate confident-sounding answers that are factually incorrect, based on outdated law, or inapplicable to your jurisdiction.

Neither a Google result nor an AI response knows the specific facts of your case, the current law in your state, or the local practices of the courts and insurance companies you are dealing with. For general orientation, these tools can be useful. For legal decisions that affect your rights and your money, they are not a substitute for an experienced personal injury attorney who practices in your state every day.

■ You Were Hit by a Drunk or Impaired Driver

As discussed in Chapter 1, crashes caused by drunk or impaired drivers carry the potential for punitive damages above and beyond standard injury compensation. Pursuing punitive damages requires specific legal strategy and trial experience. Do not attempt to handle these cases alone.

Real example: A client was hit by a drunk driver. The insurance company offered him $12,000. After I got involved and filed a lawsuit, the insurance company immediately contacted my office and paid their full six-figure policy limits. Filing the lawsuit by an experienced and reputable trial attorney was all it took. The $12,000 offer was not a good-faith evaluation of the claim — it was a test to see if my client knew any better. He did not. Until he hired the right attorney. Past results are not a guarantee of future outcomes and every case is different.

▪ How to Find and Vet the Right Attorney

Choosing the right personal injury trial attorney is one of the most important decisions you will make in your case. Here is how to do it right.

▪ Do Not Hire Based on Advertising Alone

"Friends Don't Let Friends Call TV Lawyers."

A heavy advertising presence tells you a firm has a large marketing budget. It tells you nothing about their trial record, their results, or their ability to get full value on your case. Do your homework.

The most effective personal injury trial attorneys are often not the ones with the biggest billboards or the most ads on TV.

■ Ask the Right Questions

In your initial consultation, ask every attorney these specific questions:

- How many personal injury cases have you tried to verdict in the last three years?
- Have you successfully negotiated settlements at or above policy limits?
- Have you obtained a result of $1,000,000 or more for a client?
- What percentage of your practice is personal injury?

*Any answer less than 75% is a Red Flag!

- Who specifically will be handling my case — you, or a junior associate?

Effective trial lawyers will answer "Yes" to the first three questions without hesitation. Insurance companies track which attorneys try cases and win verdicts. They pay higher settlements to lawyers they respect and fear. Hiring an attorney with a proven trial record is not just about going to court — it is about having the leverage to settle for full value without going to court.

At Fair Squared Injury Law, we can answer yes to all of these questions and 100% of our practice is personal injury work.

I have personally obtained seven-figure results for clients on numerous occasions. I tell you this not to boast, but because you deserve to know who you are hiring and what they have actually accomplished.

■ Evaluate Communication and Availability

Pay attention during the initial consultation. Does the attorney explain things clearly without rushing you? Do they answer your questions fully? Do they seem genuinely interested in your case, or are they trying to get off the phone as quickly as possible? An attorney who cannot make time for you during a consultation — when they are trying to earn your business — is unlikely to prioritize your communication needs once you are a client.

> **Ask about their case management system. Does the firm use modern legal case management software? Do clients get their own secure login to access their file documents? Can you send and receive messages through their system?**
>
> **Good personal injury firms have automated and modernized their practice specifically to enhance client communication and eliminate misunderstandings. If the attorney you are speaking with still runs paper files, seriously consider finding a different lawyer. A firm that has not embraced modern practice management tools is unlikely to have the systems, efficiency, and technological capability needed to effectively take on the multi-trillion-dollar insurance industry.**

■ Check Google Reviews and Referrals

Read Google reviews from actual clients. Look for patterns — comments about communication, responsiveness, outcomes, and how the firm treated people during a difficult time. Ask friends, family, or colleagues for referrals, but remember that personal injury is a specialized field. A referral to a general practice attorney who does not focus on personal injury is not a useful referral.

■ Understand the Fee Structure Before You Sign

Most personal injury attorneys work on a contingency fee basis, meaning they only get paid if you receive a settlement or verdict. The typical contingency fee ranges from 33.33% (one-third) pre-lawsuit up to 50% by the time a case goes through trial. Ask specifically about the percentage at each stage, and ask about any additional costs — filing fees, expert witness fees, deposition costs — and whether those come out of your portion of the recovery or are paid separately.

Get the fee structure in writing before you sign anything. Any attorney who will not provide their fee agreement in writing before you retain them is not an attorney you should hire. Period. A written fee agreement protects both of you and is standard practice for every reputable personal injury firm.

■ What Happens After You Hire an Attorney

Once you retain a personal injury attorney, your active involvement in the day-to-day management of the claim largely ends. Your attorney and their team will handle communications with the insurance companies, gather and organize your records, retain experts as needed, and manage the litigation process if a lawsuit is required.

Your responsibilities shift to attending medical appointments, responding promptly to your attorney's requests for information or documents, and being available for depositions and court appearances if your case goes to litigation. Keep your journal updated and continue telling your doctors about the ongoing impact of your injuries.

Lawsuits take time. A straightforward case that goes to litigation typically takes 18 to 24 months to resolve. Complex cases involving serious injuries, disputed liability, or difficult defendants can take three years or more. Hiring an attorney does not mean your case resolves quickly — it means your case is handled correctly and you have the best available leverage to reach a full and fair resolution.

If you have followed the steps in this book, your attorney will inherit a well-documented, well-organized case. That saves time, reduces costs, and puts your attorney in the strongest possible position from day one. The work you have done handling your own case up to this point is not wasted — it is an asset.

Chapter 11

Tools, Templates, and Resources

This chapter is your reference hub. Everything listed here supports the steps covered in this book. The templates, checklists, and resources in the Appendix at the back of this book are the same tools we use at Fair Squared Injury Law. They work for our clients. They can work for you.

Use this chapter as a quick index. When you need a specific tool, come here first.

■ Appendix A: Sample Settlement Opportunity Letter

The settlement opportunity letter is the single most important document you will submit to the insurance company. The template in Appendix A has been the core of our settlement letters at Fair Squared Injury Law for years. We have used it to recover millions of dollars for our clients.

Customize it with your specific facts, damages, and claim numbers. Do not change the structure. The structure is what makes it work.

> **The settlement letter template is not a fill-in-the-blank form. Read it carefully, understand what each section is doing, and then adapt it to your specific situation. A letter that clearly tells your human story while presenting complete and organized documentation is far more effective than a generic form letter.**

■ Appendix B: Medical Records Release Form

The HIPAA-compliant Medical Records Release Form in Appendix B is the same type of form we use at Fair Squared Injury Law. Because it is a fillable PDF form, it is provided as a free standalone download rather than printed in this book. Download your free copy at www.Fair2Law.com/downloads. It will work for nearly all of your records requests. Some providers require their own specific form — if a provider insists on their own version, use theirs. For everyone else, our form is sufficient.

> **TIP: Your medical providers are required by law to provide you with a complete copy of your medical billing and records upon written request. In many cases you can pick up your billing ledger and records the same day you request them. Do not let any provider tell you otherwise.**

■ Appendix C: Pain and Activity Journal Templates

Appendix C contains sample journal and activity log sheets. These are the starting point for documenting your non-economic damages — the human cost of the crash. As discussed in Chapter 9, specific and consistent journal entries are among the most powerful evidence you can create for your case.

Use the templates as a guide, but write in your own voice. Your journal should sound like you, not like a legal document. The more human and specific your entries are, the more persuasive they will be.

■ Appendix D: Documentation Checklist

The documentation checklist in Appendix D covers everything you need to gather before sending your settlement demand. Use it to make sure nothing is missing before you submit. A complete, organized submission gets taken more seriously and processed faster than a disorganized or incomplete one.

The checklist covers:

- Police report and crash details
- Photos of the crash scene, all vehicles involved, and vehicle interiors
- Photos of your injuries — taken at the scene and at intervals during your recovery

- Medical bills from every treatment provider, in itemized format with billing codes
- Medical records from every treatment provider
- Radiologist reports for all imaging studies
- Electronic copies of your actual imaging files if available
- Lost wage documentation:
    - Employer letter confirming missed dates, hourly rate or salary, and total loss
    - Spreadsheet showing missed hours/days, hourly wage, and total lost wages
    - Records of any sick leave, PTO, or vacation time used
- Claim numbers for every insurance claim involved:
    - Bodily Injury / Liability (at-fault insurer)
    - Property Damage (at-fault insurer)
    - Medical Payments / PIP (your insurance)
    - Uninsured / Underinsured Motorist (your insurance)
    - Health insurance subrogation (your health insurer)
- Copies of your pain journal and activity logs
- Written statements from family, friends, or coworkers documenting observed changes in your daily life

Put your claim number on every document you submit. Every page. Every email. Every fax. Insurance companies handle thousands of claims simultaneously. A missing claim number is one of the most common reasons documents get lost or delayed. Make it the first thing on every page.

■ Appendix E: Communications Log

The Communications Log is a structured, multi-part form for recording every interaction with every insurance company from the day of the crash through final settlement. Because of its size and formatting — including wide tracking tables best viewed in landscape orientation — it is provided as a free standalone download rather than printed in this book.

Download your free copy at www.Fair2Law.com/downloads. Print as many copies as you need.

The log includes seven parts: your crash and personal information, key contacts, a full communications log with an example entry, a recorded statement request tracker, a letters and emails log, a medical appointments tracker, and an out-of-pocket expenses log with running total.

> **Insurance companies will sometimes tell you they said or agreed to something that never happened. A complete communications log shuts that down immediately. It is also an invaluable asset if you eventually hire an attorney — they will not have to repeat work you have already done, which saves time and money. Start the log the day of the crash and never stop updating it.**

■ Online Resources

The following online resources may be useful as you navigate your claim. As with all online information, verify that what you find is current and applicable to your state. Do not rely on any website as a substitute for legal advice from a licensed personal injury attorney in your jurisdiction.

- National Association of Insurance Commissioners (NAIC) — naic.org. Provides links to every state insurance department. Use it to file complaints, check insurer licensing, and find your state's specific insurance regulations.

- Your State Department of Insurance — Search "[Your State] Department of Insurance." Most states allow you to verify insurer licensing, file complaints, and access consumer guides specific to your state's laws.
- Your State DMV or Department of Transportation — Many states allow online accident report filing for minor crashes not handled by police. Check your state's DMV or DOT website for online reporting options.
- Fair Health Consumer — fairhealthconsumer.org. Helps you understand medical billing and typical costs for specific treatments and procedures. Useful when disputing whether a medical bill is reasonable.
- 988 Suicide and Crisis Lifeline — Call or text 988. If the emotional and psychological impact of your crash becomes overwhelming, help is available immediately. You are not alone.

Be cautious with legal information found online, including on attorney websites. Laws vary significantly by state and change frequently. A blog post written for a California audience may be completely inapplicable in Colorado or Wyoming. When in doubt, call a licensed personal injury attorney in your state. Most offer free consultations and will answer basic questions at no charge.

■ A Final Note

You have now read everything this book has to offer. If you have followed the steps in these chapters — documented your injuries, organized your records, communicated strategically with the insurance companies, and built your human story — you are in a far stronger position than the vast majority of people who handle their own claims.

If at any point the process becomes overwhelming, the insurance company stops dealing fairly, or your injuries turn out to be more serious than you initially realized — call us. We offer free consultations. We will tell you honestly whether you need us. And if you do, we will fight for every dollar you are owed.

Fair Squared Injury Law

56 Inverness Drive East, Suite 235

Englewood, Colorado 80112

Phone: (720) 645-1123

Website: www.Fair2Law.com

Fax: (720) 794-3318

Justice Elevated.

About the Author

Glenn B. Fair, Esq. is a personal injury trial attorney and the founder of Fair Squared Injury Law, based in Englewood, Colorado.

Before becoming a lawyer, Glenn spent 22 years in law enforcement, including work in internal affairs investigations — experience that gave him an unmatched ability to investigate crashes, identify liability, and recognize when insurance companies are not dealing in good faith. He has also worked in the casino industry, where reading people and understanding negotiation dynamics are survival skills.

Glenn has obtained seven-figure results for clients on numerous occasions. He takes cases to trial — not as a last resort, but as a core part of his practice — because he believes the only real leverage against insurance companies is a lawyer they know will walk into a courtroom and win.

He was a car crash victim himself. He knows what it feels like to sit on your side of the table.

Glenn is licensed to practice law in Colorado and Wyoming. He is married to Evynne, and together they are building the Fair Squared brand — which also includes Fair Squared Vehicle Vault and Fair Squared Racing.

Did This Book Help You?

If this book helped you navigate your case, protect your rights, or simply gave you the confidence to deal with the insurance company on equal footing — that is exactly why it was written.

We ask for two things in return:

1. Leave us a 5-Star Google Review.

Our business is built on referrals and on being of genuine service to others. A review takes two minutes and helps the next person who needs this information find us.

Leave a 5-Star Review for Fair Squared Injury Law:

https://g.page/r/Cc2jTMFG4_ObEB0/review

2. Tell someone who needs this.

If you know someone who has been in a crash and does not know where to start, give them this book or tell them where to find it. You may be the reason they do not get taken advantage of.

When You Need More Than a Book

Some cases cannot be handled alone — and this book has been honest with you about exactly when that line gets crossed.

If the insurance company is lowballing you, disputing liability, refusing to budge, or your injuries are serious — call us. We offer free consultations, we will tell you straight whether you need a lawyer, and if you do, we will fight for every dollar you are owed.

Fair Squared Injury Law

56 Inverness Drive East, Suite 235

Englewood, Colorado 80112

Phone: (720) 645-1123

Website: www.Fair2Law.com

Fax: (720) 794-3318

Free Consultations

Follow Glenn: @injuryattorneyglenn

Instagram

Follow Evynne: @legalEfair

Instagram

Fair Squared Injury Law

Justice Elevated.

APPENDIX A

Settlement Opportunity Letter — Template

Fill in all fields shown in blue. Delete instructions in brackets before sending.

CLAIM NUMBER:

[INSERT CLAIM NUMBER — put this on every page]

CLEAR AND UNEQUIVOCAL TIME SENSITIVE DEMAND TO SETTLE FOR GLOBAL POLICY LIMITS AND TO PROTECT [AT-FAULT DRIVER NAME] FROM HAVING TO ENDURE THE STRESS, INCONVENIENCE, AND CONSEQUENCES OF LITIGATION AND JURY VERDICT/JUDGMENT IN EXCESS OF THE POLICY LIMITS.

THIS DEMAND EXPIRES ON [DAY OF WEEK], [DATE] AT 4:00 P.M. [YOUR TIME ZONE] TIME.

Dear

[AT-FAULT DRIVER NAME], [INSURANCE COMPANY NAME], all real parties in interest, all Insurance Company Decision Makers and All Money Decision-Makers:

Please accept this as a time sensitive, clear and unequivocal global policy limits demand. Please forward this demand to all above listed persons. Let us be clear that this settlement demand is for whatever the global policy limits are. I will sign a full and final release of all claims against your insured in return for the payment of this demand within the stated timeframe.

This unequivocal time sensitive demand expires on **[Day of week], [Date]** at 4:00 P.M. **[Your Time Zone]** time and if it is not accepted prior to its expiration, we will consider the policy to be open. Acceptance of this demand is also expressly conditioned upon: the receipt of payment within 14 days of acceptance; the liability insurance carrier(s) providing me with proof of all applicable policy limits; and consent to settle from uninsured/underinsured carriers. Please respond in writing as this is the only response method which will be considered.

THE CRASH AND WHAT HAPPENED

[Describe what caused the crash — who did what, where, when. Be factual and brief. 2-4 sentences.]

[Describe what happened immediately during and after impact — forces involved, vehicle damage, airbags, what you felt.]

[State what medical facility you went to on the day of the crash and whether you arrived by ambulance.]

[Describe the injuries you suffered as documented in your medical records.]

THE HUMAN IMPACT

[Describe what your friends, family, and/or coworkers witnessed — how the crash changed your daily life, your relationships, and your ability to do the things you did before.]

[List the types of medical providers you saw — e.g., emergency room, M.D., pain management, chiropractor, physical therapist. Do not list every visit — those are in the records enclosed.]

Please make sure that all money decision-makers and [AT-FAULT DRIVER NAME] immediately read this demand. Further, inform [AT-FAULT DRIVER NAME] that this stressful experience can be avoided if [his/her/their] insurance company pays the full limits of the policy — a policy which [AT-FAULT DRIVER NAME] pays good money for.

Please ensure [AT-FAULT DRIVER NAME] receives a copy of this demand so [he/she/they] can both: instruct **[Insurance Company Name]** to pay the policy limits so [AT-FAULT DRIVER NAME]'s family and assets will be protected, and to give **[AT-FAULT DRIVER NAME]** the opportunity to retain private counsel to protect **[his/her/their]** personal interests. This time sensitive unequivocal settlement demand is for whatever **[AT-FAULT DRIVER NAME]**'s policy limits might be.

The bottom line is that I sincerely want to provide an opportunity to resolve this case for an amount of money that does not require

[AT-FAULT DRIVER NAME] to pay a single penny over what **[his/her/their]** insurance coverage is.

DAMAGES CALCULATION

My demand is for payment of every single dollar of damages as allowed by law. I have had **[describe your injuries and pain from the date of the crash to the date they resolved or to the present]**. This is **[NUMBER OF DAYS]** days. By the time this demand expires, I will have endured **[NUMBER OF DAYS]** days of inconvenience, emotional stress, and impairment to the quality of my life as a result of this crash.

The global policy limits are quite easily exceeded when we multiply my **[NUMBER OF DAYS]** days of injury and harm by 16 hours per day, then multiply by **[YOUR HOURLY WAGE]** per hour, then multiply the resulting total by each of the following damages (delete any that do not apply to your case):

- Physical and mental pain and suffering;
- Inconvenience;
- Emotional stress;
- Loss of enjoyment of the quality of life;
- Physical impairment; and
- Disfigurement.

It is imperative that you understand that there is no civil law or jury instruction anywhere that says money justice for damages in my case should be little, or cheap.

Enclosed please find my medical bills and medical records that show my complaints and reasons for seeking medical care and undergoing treatment following this crash.

Please know that any request for an extension of this demand will constitute a rejection of the clear and unequivocal settlement opportunity. You are being given more than enough time to evaluate this case and make a settlement offer.

Please contact me with your response or any questions by email only. My email address is: [YOUR EMAIL ADDRESS].

Respectfully yours,

[YOUR FULL NAME]

[YOUR MAILING ADDRESS]

[YOUR EMAIL ADDRESS]

[YOUR PHONE NUMBER]

APPENDIX E1

Completed Example of Settlement Letter — Sent by Attorney

This is a real letter used by Fair Squared Injury Law, included here for context only.

References to lawsuits and litigation have been removed from the template (Appendix A) you should be using. This example is provided so you can see how the letter reads when completed by a licensed attorney.

CLEAR AND UNEQUIVOCAL TIME SENSITIVE DEMAND TO SETTLE FOR GLOBAL POLICY LIMITS AND TO PROTECT [AT-FAULT DRIVER NAME] FROM HAVING TO ENDURE THE STRESS, INCONVENIENCE, AND CONSEQUENCES OF LITIGATION AND JURY VERDICT/JUDGMENT IN EXCESS OF THE POLICY LIMITS.

THIS DEMAND EXPIRES ON MONDAY, OCTOBER 4, 2020 AT 5:00 P.M. MOUNTAIN TIME.

Dear [AT-FAULT DRIVER NAME], [At-Fault Driver's Insurance Company], all real parties in interest, all Insurance Company Decision Makers and All Money Decision-Makers:

Please accept this as a time sensitive, clear and unequivocal global policy limits demand on behalf of our clients (hereinafter "Injured Family"). Please forward this demand to all above listed persons. Let us be clear that this settlement demand is for whatever the global policy limits are. The Injured Family will sign a full and final release of all claims against your insured in return for the payment of this demand within the stated timeframe.

This unequivocal time sensitive demand expires on Monday, October 4, 2020, at 4:00 P.M. Mountain Time and if it is not accepted prior to its expiration, we will consider the policy to be open. Acceptance of this demand is also expressly conditioned upon: the receipt of payment within 14 days of acceptance; the liability insurance carrier(s) providing us with proof of all applicable policy limits; and consent to settle from uninsured/underinsured carriers. Please respond in writing as this is the only response method which will be considered.

Failure to pay this demand will result in our law firm moving forward to a very public jury trial. The public trial will needlessly expose [AT-FAULT DRIVER NAME] to reliving the horror and stress of the poor choices they made on the day of the crash. They will also be forced to be present in court and will face days of testimony about how [AT-FAULT DRIVER NAME]'s actions severely harmed the Injured Family. The trial will also expose [AT-FAULT DRIVER NAME] to the risk of an excess jury verdict and publicly recorded judgment against them in excess of the policy limits.

The Injured Family does not want to go through litigation. They are not a greedy, lawsuit-happy family. The Injured Family is a nice family from [CITY] who were on their way to church when [AT-FAULT DRIVER NAME] slammed into their stopped vehicle at over 50 MPH.

The impact of the crash was so severe that it slammed the Injured Family backwards into their seats and then forward against their seatbelts and airbags when their vehicle was forced into the vehicle in front of them. The speeds were so high that the Injured Family's vehicle careened off of the vehicle in front of them and into the intersection. The family's vehicle was then sideswiped by another passing car and forced into the oncoming traffic lanes. The family was transported to the hospital by ambulance where they received trauma care for their injuries.

The police responded to the crash and the scene and damage was well documented. See the attached photos of the client's obvious injuries, including the blood on their child's clothing (*photos omitted from this book to protect client privacy*).

The Injured Family's co-workers, family, friends, and clergy will testify at trial to the physical and emotional trauma suffered by the family due to [AT-FAULT DRIVER NAME]'s negligence.

If [At-Fault Driver's Insurance Company] forces the Injured Family to move forward with litigation, we will be asking a jury for much more than the global policy limits. Please make sure that all money decision-makers and [AT-FAULT DRIVER NAME] immediately read this demand. Further, inform [AT-FAULT DRIVER NAME] that this stressful and humiliating experience can be avoided if [At-Fault Driver's Insurance Company] pays the full limits of the insurance policy — a policy which [AT-FAULT DRIVER NAME] pays good money for.

Please ensure [AT-FAULT DRIVER NAME] receives a copy of this demand so they can both: instruct [At-Fault Driver's Insurance Company] to pay the policy limits so [AT-FAULT DRIVER NAME]'s family and assets will be protected, and to give [AT-FAULT DRIVER NAME] the opportunity to retain private counsel to protect their personal interests. This time sensitive unequivocal settlement demand is for whatever [AT-FAULT DRIVER NAME]'s policy limits might be.

The bottom line is that the Injured Family sincerely wants to provide an opportunity to resolve this case for an amount of money that does not require [AT-FAULT DRIVER NAME] to pay a single penny over what their insurance coverage is.

The Injured Family's demand is for payment of every single dollar of damages as allowed by law. In determining such damages, you shall consider any noneconomic losses or injuries which the Injured Family has had to the present time or which they will probably have in the future, including: physical and mental pain and suffering, inconvenience, emotional stress, and impairment of the quality of life.

It is imperative that you understand that there is no civil law or jury instruction anywhere that says money justice for damages in the Injured Family's civil case should be little, or cheap.

The Injured Family's Driver had neck and back pain from the day of the crash until their symptoms resolved on or about [DATE OF HEALING]. This is 208 days. By the time this time sensitive, unequivocal demand for global policy limits expires, Injured Family's Driver will have endured a total of 208 days of inconvenience, emotional stress, and impairment to the quality of his life as a result of the crash.

What should quickly become clear to you is that the global policy limits are quite easily exceeded when we multiply the Injured Family's days of injury and harms by 16 hours a day (assuming they sleep 8 hours pain free — they don't), then multiply the 16 hours per day by $15.16 per hour (state minimum wage), and then multiply the resulting total by each of the following damages:

- Past and future physical and mental pain and suffering;
- Past and future inconvenience;
- Past and future emotional stress;
- Past and future impairment of the quality of life;
- Past and future physical impairment; and
- Past and future disfigurement as Front Passenger Injured Family member has scars on their face from cuts sustained in the crash.

After the economic damages of over $100,000 are added to the non-economic damages, there is zero question that the policy limits are exceeded. Rest assured, if this unequivocal demand is not paid, we will be asking a jury for much, much more than this amount. To be crystal clear, the Injured Family hereby demands full compensation for all damages caused by the negligence of [AT-FAULT DRIVER NAME].

Enclosed, please find the emergency room and ambulance bills and medical records that show the Injured Family's complaints and reasons for seeking medical care and having to undergo imaging and other tests in the ER since [AT-FAULT DRIVER NAME] slammed into the Injured Family's vehicle injuring all of them. The family also has bills from conservative care providers such as chiropractic, physical therapy, and pediatrician. These bills have not been provided as the ER billing and non-economic damages alone justify a global policy limits tender.

Please know that any request for an extension of this demand will constitute a rejection of the clear and unequivocal settlement opportunity. [At-Fault Driver's Insurance Company] is being given more than enough time to evaluate this case and knows that the risk of a jury verdict and judgment in excess of the policy limits is very serious.

Sincerely,

Attorney at Law
Fair Squared Injury Law
(720) 645-1123 | www.Fair2Law.com

APPENDIX C

Personal Injury Daily Journal

Print as many copies of the journal page as you need.

This journal helps you document how your injury affects your daily life. Fill it out each day as best you can. There are no right or wrong answers — just be honest and specific. Specific, dated entries are far more persuasive to insurance companies and juries than vague generalizations. Write about what actually happened to you today. And when you go to your next medical appointment, tell your doctor what you wrote here.

IMPORTANT REMINDERS:

- Write only about crash-related impacts.
- Be specific and honest. Do not exaggerate.
- Document good days AND bad days — including what you tried and how you paid for it afterward.
- Tell your doctor at every appointment what you wrote in your journal.
- Your journal may become part of your case and could be reviewed by the insurance company or in court.
- Write every entry as though someone else will read it someday — because they might.

DATE: ________________________

OVERALL TODAY: ○ Bad day ○ Difficult day ○ Mixed ○ Better day

Pain Level Today (circle one):

0 1 2 3 4 5 6 7 8 9 10

0 = No pain | 5 = Moderate | 10 = Worst pain imaginable

Where do you feel pain today?

Describe the pain (circle all that apply):

○ Sharp ○ Dull ○ Aching ○ Burning ○ Throbbing ○ Shooting ○ Tingling/Numbness

Other: ______________________________

What activities were difficult or impossible today? Be specific.

Example: "I tried to vacuum. Had to stop after 10 minutes. Took 45 minutes total."

Good or low-pain day? What did you try, and what happened in the days after?

Example: "Hiked 2 miles (normally 5+). Was significantly sorer for 3 days afterward."

How did your injury affect your relationships today?

Include spouse/partner, children, friends. Include physical intimacy if applicable.

Did you miss anything important today because of your injury?

How did you feel emotionally today?

○ Frustrated ○ Anxious ○ Depressed ○ Angry ○ Fearful (driving) ○ Okay

Other: ______________________________

How did you sleep last night?

○ Slept well ○ Woke from pain ○ Difficulty getting comfortable ○ Very poor sleep

Medication or treatment today:

Did you tell your doctor about anything from this entry?

○ Yes — what: ____________________________________

○ No

○ No appointment yet

Anything else to note about today:

Justice Elevated.

DATE: ________________________

OVERALL TODAY: ○ Bad day ○ Difficult day ○ Mixed ○ Better day

Pain Level Today (circle one):

0 1 2 3 4 5 6 7 8 9 10

0 = No pain | 5 = Moderate | 10 = Worst pain imaginable

Where do you feel pain today?

Describe the pain (circle all that apply):

○ Sharp ○ Dull ○ Aching ○ Burning ○ Throbbing ○ Shooting ○ Tingling/Numbness

Other: ______________________________

What activities were difficult or impossible today? Be specific.

Example: "I tried to vacuum. Had to stop after 10 minutes. Took 45 minutes total."

Good or low-pain day? What did you try, and what happened in the days after?

Example: "Hiked 2 miles (normally 5+). Was significantly sorer for 3 days afterward."

How did your injury affect your relationships today?

Include spouse/partner, children, friends. Include physical intimacy if applicable.

Did you miss anything important today because of your injury?

How did you feel emotionally today?

○ Frustrated ○ Anxious ○ Depressed ○ Angry ○ Fearful (driving) ○ Okay

Other: ______________________________

How did you sleep last night?

○ Slept well ○ Woke from pain ○ Difficulty getting comfortable ○ Very poor sleep

---

Medication or treatment today:

Did you tell your doctor about anything from this entry?

○ Yes — what: ___________________________________

○ No

○ No appointment yet

Anything else to note about today:

Fair Squared Injury Law | (720) 645-1123 | www.Fair2Law.com | Free Consultations

56 Inverness Drive East, Suite 235, Englewood, Colorado 80112

Justice Elevated.

DATE: ________________________

OVERALL TODAY: ○ Bad day ○ Difficult day ○ Mixed ○ Better day

Pain Level Today (circle one):

0 1 2 3 4 5 6 7 8 9 10

0 = No pain | 5 = Moderate | 10 = Worst pain imaginable

Where do you feel pain today?

Describe the pain (circle all that apply):

○ Sharp ○ Dull ○ Aching ○ Burning ○ Throbbing ○ Shooting ○ Tingling/Numbness

Other: ______________________________

What activities were difficult or impossible today? Be specific.

Example: "I tried to vacuum. Had to stop after 10 minutes. Took 45 minutes total."

Good or low-pain day? What did you try, and what happened in the days after?

Example: "Hiked 2 miles (normally 5+). Was significantly sorer for 3 days afterward."

How did your injury affect your relationships today?

Include spouse/partner, children, friends. Include physical intimacy if applicable.

Did you miss anything important today because of your injury?

How did you feel emotionally today?

○ Frustrated ○ Anxious ○ Depressed ○ Angry ○ Fearful (driving) ○ Okay

Other: ______________________________

How did you sleep last night?

○ Slept well ○ Woke from pain ○ Difficulty getting comfortable ○ Very poor sleep

---

Medication or treatment today:

Did you tell your doctor about anything from this entry?

○ Yes — what: ___________________________________

○ No

- No appointment yet

Anything else to note about today:

Fair Squared Injury Law | (720) 645-1123 | www.Fair2Law.com | Free Consultations

56 Inverness Drive East, Suite 235, Englewood, Colorado 80112

Justice Elevated.

APPENDIX D

Documentation Checklist

Work through this checklist in order. Check each item only when it is fully complete.

AT THE SCENE — CHAPTERS 2 & 3

Safety

☐ Assessed surroundings for immediate hazards — traffic, fire, fuel leaks

☐ Checked on passengers and other drivers

☐ Moved vehicles off the roadway if safe to do so

☐ Turned on hazard lights

☐ Deployed warning devices (cones, flares) if available and safe

Emergency Response

☐ Called 911

☐ Provided dispatcher with: location, number of vehicles, injuries, hazards

☐ Requested ambulance if needed

At the Scene — Police

☐ Gave factual, brief statement to responding officer — no speculation

☐ Described injuries honestly — did NOT say "I am fine" or "I am not hurt"

⚠ *Say: "I feel shaken up. My neck is sore. I will see a doctor after I leave."*

☐ Declined to provide a written statement to police

☐ Obtained crash report number

☐ Obtained officer's name, badge number, and contact information

Documentation at the Scene

☐ Photographed all vehicles from multiple angles

☐ Photographed license plates of all vehicles

☐ Photographed other driver's license, insurance card, and registration

☐ Photographed road conditions, skid marks, debris, traffic signs

☐ Photographed weather and visibility conditions

☐ Photographed interior of your vehicle (deployed airbags, damage)

☐ Photographed your visible injuries

☐ Recorded video walkthrough of scene if safe

☐ Confirmed location services were enabled on phone (timestamps and geotags)

Witness Information

☐ Identified all available witnesses

☐ Collected witness names, phone numbers, and email addresses

☐ Obtained brief written or recorded statement from each witness if possible

Other Driver Information

☐ Exchanged full name and contact information

☐ Exchanged driver's license number and state of issue

☐ Exchanged insurance company name and policy number

☐ Exchanged vehicle registration information

After the Scene — Same Day

☐ Written personal account of the crash completed same day

> ⚠ *Include: sequence of events, road/weather conditions, signal status, your speed, other driver's actions, statements made at scene*

IMMEDIATE POST-CRASH STEPS — CHAPTER 5

Vehicle Location — Both Insurers

☐ Called at-fault insurance company and provided vehicle location

⚠ Storage fees: $75-$150/day. Must notify both carriers immediately.

☐ Called your own insurance company and provided vehicle location

☐ Documented name, date, and time of each call

Your Own Insurance Company

☐ Set up claim with your own insurer

☐ Provided crash date, time, location, police report number, and vehicle descriptions

☐ Provided photos and witness information

☐ Gave recorded statement (required by your contract)

☐ Signed medical releases requested by your own insurer

☐ Instructed your insurer in writing not to share information with the at-fault insurer

At-Fault Insurance Company

☐ Set up claim with the at-fault insurer

☐ Provided basic crash information only — date, location, police report number

☐ Declined recorded statement to at-fault adjuster

☐ Declined to sign any medical releases for at-fault insurer

☐ Disclosed Medicare status if applicable

⚠ REQUIRED: You must disclose to the at-fault insurer whether you are on Medicare.

☐ Asked about policy limits — used exact phrase: "Is this a state minimum policy?"

Health Insurance

☐ Sent written notification letter to health insurance carrier

> ⚠ *Letter must include: your name, member ID, primary insured name if not you, crash date, injured body parts, your contact information*

☐ Kept copy of letter and proof of mailing

Medicare / Medicaid

☐ If on Medicare or Medicaid — contacted a personal injury attorney before proceeding

> ⚠ *Do not attempt to navigate Medicare/Medicaid repayment rules without legal help.*

Communication Log Started (Appendix E)

☐ Created written log for all insurance communications

> ⚠ *Log each contact: date, time, name, company, department, summary of discussion*

MEDICAL CARE — CHAPTER 4

Immediate Medical Care

☐ Went to ER or urgent care immediately after leaving the crash scene

☐ Told all medical staff about every symptom — no minimizing

☐ Disclosed all pre-existing conditions so doctors could distinguish them from crash injuries

☐ Asked for complete medical records before leaving — not just discharge summary

Follow-Up Care

☐ Scheduled follow-up appointments immediately

☐ Attended every scheduled appointment

☐ Followed every doctor's care plan

☐ Reported any new symptoms or worsening pain to doctor immediately

Six-Week Assessment

☐ Assessed pain improvement at six weeks of treatment

☐ If no improvement — requested imaging (MRI) from treating doctor

☐ If doctor declined imaging — sought second opinion from crash injury specialist

⚠ *Do not continue indefinite conservative care without a specific diagnosis.*

BUILDING YOUR CASE — CHAPTER 6

Medical Records Collection

☐ Requested itemized billing ledger from every treating provider

⚠ *Request billing codes — the bills mailed to your home are not sufficient.*

☐ Requested complete medical records from every treating provider

☐ Requested radiologist reports for all imaging studies

☐ Saved all pharmacy receipts for crash-related medications

☐ For ER visit — requested three separate bills:

- ☐ Hospital bill
- ☐ Treating physicians' bill
- ☐ Radiologist's bill

☐ For ER visit — requested medical records from:

- ☐ Hospital (full records including nursing notes, lab work, imaging)
- ☐ Radiologist (imaging interpretation report)

⚠ *Treating physicians are generally part of the hospital ER record.*

File Organization

☐ Set up dedicated digital file for all crash-related documents

☐ Organized all records and bills chronologically — ER first, then each subsequent visit

☐ Created medical appointment log/spreadsheet with: date, provider, diagnosis/treatment, cost

☐ Backed up all digital files to secure cloud storage

Medical Records Redaction

☐ Reviewed all records and identified unrelated items to redact

☐ Redacted using Adobe Acrobat or equivalent PDF tool — NOT a black marker

☐ Verified redacted content is permanently removed and cannot be recovered

> ⚠ *Remove: family history, unrelated conditions, unrelated body parts, unrelated visits*

Lost Wage Documentation

☐ Obtained pay stubs and W-2s from prior two years

☐ Obtained written employer letter confirming: missed dates, hourly rate/salary, typical hours

☐ Documented all sick leave, PTO, and vacation time used

☐ Created spreadsheet: missed dates x hours x hourly wage = total lost wages

☐ Documented career impacts beyond lost wages: missed promotions, lost clients, performance issues

> ⚠ *Do not provide tax returns to insurer without consulting an attorney first.*

Visual Evidence — Ongoing

☐ Continued photographing injuries over time — bruising, swelling, scarring

☐ Photographed any permanent changes to body after healing complete

☐ Recorded periodic video updates showing impact of injuries on daily activities

☐ Created dedicated photo/video folder with dated, labeled files

⚠ Never edit, filter, crop, or enhance any evidence photos or videos.

Journal — Started and Maintained

☐ Started pain and activity journal

☐ Writing regular dated entries — specific, personal, honest

☐ Documenting bad pain days: hour-by-hour impact

☐ Documenting good/low-pain days: what was attempted, what had to stop, days of increased pain afterward

☐ Documenting relationship impacts — including physical intimacy

☐ Documenting career impacts

☐ Documenting mental health changes

☐ Reporting journal entries to treating doctors at appointments

⚠ Your journal will become part of your case. Write only crash-related content. Everything should be true.

Third-Party Statements

☐ Asked family, friends, or coworkers for written statements about observed changes

⚠ Statements should be specific, honest, and describe who you were before vs. after.

CALCULATING YOUR CASE VALUE — CHAPTERS 9 & 10

Economic Damages

☐ Totaled all medical bills

☐ Totaled all lost wages

☐ Totaled all mileage to/from medical appointments

☐ Totaled all out-of-pocket expenses

☐ Totaled all co-pays and deductibles

Non-Economic Damages — Per Diem Calculation

☐ Determined hourly wage at time of crash

☐ Calculated daily rate: hourly wage x 16 hours

☐ Determined number of days of significant pain and limitation

☐ Calculated non-economic damages: daily rate x number of days

> ⚠ *This is your floor, not your ceiling. A trial attorney may calculate significantly more.*

Subrogation Obligations

☐ Contacted health insurer for final subrogation amount in writing

☐ Contacted MedPay insurer for final subrogation amount in writing

☐ Contacted Medicare/Medicaid if applicable (with attorney assistance)

☐ Totaled all subrogation obligations

Walk-Away Amount

☐ Calculated walk-away amount: total settlement needed minus all payback obligations

> ⚠ *Do not accept a settlement that leaves you below your walk-away amount.*

SETTLEMENT DEMAND — CHAPTER 10

☐ Reached maximum medical improvement before sending demand

☐ Confirmed UM/UIM consent to settle — obtained written permission from own insurer

☐ Drafted settlement opportunity letter including:

- ☐ Opening: crash date, location, claim number
- ☐ Summary of crash and liability (2-3 sentences max)
- ☐ Brief injury and treatment statement

- ☐ Non-economic damages description drawn from journal
- ☐ Demand for full global available policy limits
- ☐ 35-day response deadline
- ☐ Your mailing address and email address

☐ Assembled complete submission package:

- ☐ Settlement letter
- ☐ Police report
- ☐ All medical bills (itemized)
- ☐ All medical records (redacted)
- ☐ Lost wage documentation
- ☐ Photos and visual evidence
- ☐ Journal excerpts if appropriate

☐ Put claim number on every single document

☐ Submitted by email, fax, or insurer upload portal — NOT by mail

☐ Sent same package to own insurer simultaneously

☐ Followed up by email to confirm receipt

☐ Logged submission date and confirmation in communication log

NEGOTIATION AND SETTLEMENT — CHAPTERS 8 & 10

☐ Waited for response within 35-day deadline

☐ Evaluated initial offer against total claim value and walk-away amount

☐ If lowball offer — prepared written counteroffer (not verbal)

⚠ *Three-offer method: set final number, add 50% for offer 2, add 50% again for offer 1.*

☐ Never revealed final number before third offer

☐ Requested written explanation of insurer's valuation if offer remained low

☐ Resisted artificial deadlines — only the Statute of Limitations is real

☐ Know the Statute of Limitations in your state

☐ If insurance company refuses to move — contacted experienced personal injury trial attorney

Accepting the Settlement

☐ Received written settlement agreement

☐ Verified agreement includes: amount, who pays medical bills/subrogation, payment deadline, specific claims released

☐ Did NOT sign until all terms are confirmed in writing

☐ Consulted attorney to review agreement if any terms were unclear

Final Distribution

☐ Obtained final subrogation amounts in writing from all payees

⚠ These letters expire — typically 30 days. Move promptly.

☐ Paid all medical providers with outstanding balances

☐ Paid all subrogation obligations

☐ Paid remaining co-pays and deductibles

☐ Paid by check or credit card — kept proof of every payment

☐ Consulted tax professional regarding taxability of settlement

⚠ WARNING: Medicare and Medicaid MUST be repaid. Failure = denial of future benefits and legal action.

STOP AND CALL A LAWYER IF ANY OF THE FOLLOWING APPLY

☐ Serious injuries: surgery, herniated disk, TBI, permanent disability

☐ The at-fault driver was drunk or impaired

☐ Liability is disputed — insurer is claiming you are partially at fault

☐ Bad faith tactics: unreasonable delays, denial without basis, misrepresented coverage

☐ Settlement offer does not cover medical bills plus fair non-economic damages

☐ You are on Medicare or Medicaid

☐ Complex legal rules: comparative fault, UM/UIM disputes, SOL concerns

☐ You feel overwhelmed or uncertain at any point in this process

Fair Squared Injury Law | (720) 645-1123 | www.Fair2Law.com | Free Consultations

56 Inverness Drive East, Suite 235, Englewood, Colorado 80112

Justice Elevated.

www.ingramcontent.com/pod-product-compliance
Lightning Source LLC
LaVergne TN
LVHW090611110826
845146LV00001B/347